MW01516131

Careers in Focus

Energy

Ferguson Publishing Company
Chicago, Illinois

Andrew Morkes, *Managing Editor-Career Publications*
Carol Yehling, *Senior Editor*
Anne Paterson, *Editor*
Nora Walsh, *Assistant Editor*

Copyright © 2002 Ferguson Publishing Company

Library of Congress Cataloging-in-Publication Data

Careers in focus. Energy.
    p. cm. -- (Careers in focus)
  ISBN 0-89434-402-1
  1. Energy industries--Vocational guidance. I. Title. II. Series.
  TJ163.2 .C367 2001
  333.79'023--dc21

                                        2001003267

Printed in the United States of America

Cover photo courtesy Lester Lefkowitz/The Stock Market

Published and distributed by
Ferguson Publishing Company
200 West Jackson Boulevard, 7th Floor
Chicago, Illinois 60606
800-306-9941
www.fergpubco.com

All rights reserved. No part of this publication may be reproduced, stored in a retrieval system, or transmitted by any means, electronic, mechanical, photocopying or otherwise, without the prior permission of the publisher.

Y-9

Table of Contents

Introduction

Nearly every field of science and engineering is involved in the energy industry. Among the oil industry's key employees are geologists, geophysicists, petroleum engineers, chemists, and chemical engineers. Together, these highly skilled men and women carry much of the responsibility for finding oil, producing it, processing it in the refinery, and conducting petroleum research.

The U.S. oil industry comprises thousands of companies engaged in one or more of five principal categories: exploration, production, refining, transportation, and marketing. Companies that are active in all five are known as "integrated" companies.

Mineralogists and paleontologists who study fossil remains in the earth as a clue to oil-bearing sands are among the scientists who perform exploration research. According to one expert, the chances of striking oil when a well is drilled average only one in nine. Only one in 144 wells drilled in new fields results in commercially significant quantities of oil and natural gas.

Geologists use a variety of sources to help find petroleum. A geologist will, for instance, use background information to hunt for signs of certain kinds of underground rock formations where oil is likely to collect. For example, oil may be found where layers of certain kinds of rocks have slipped or tilted in a particular way, or where the layers have been pushed up to form a kind of underground "dome." Sometimes geologists can find places where the tilted layers stick out of the earth. They frequently drill holes to get core samples of the underground layers.

Geophysicists rely on another important type of exploration method. Working with such tools as the gravimeter, magnetometer, and seismograph, they chart underground rock formations and calculate the composition, depth, thickness, and slope of the structures. In the past, these calculations were made with explosives, set off at several different points.

Later developments in seismic land surveys include the use of vibratory or percussion devices that do away with the drilling of holes and the use of explosives. With vibratory devices, the geophysicist can get accurate information and minimize environmental damage. In water, these devices send out pulses in the form of electrical discharges or contained explosions of propane gas or air so that marine life won't be harmed.

Petroleum and natural gas often are found in the same fields. When the geologist and the geophysicist have turned in their reports and recommendations, a petroleum company decides whether to drill. Drilling requires a great amount of equipment and supplies. Dozens of skilled workers are required, including exploration crew, geologists, drilling crew, engineers, and other skilled technicians. Once recovered, the crude oil has to be transported to refineries where it is turned into thousands of useful products.

Gas energy comes from domestic natural gas wells. Gas production has been bolstered by pipeline imports from Canada, by domestic production of synthetic natural gas from petroleum, and by delivery of liquefied natural gas by ship from overseas. Potential sources for future use include natural gas from Alaska and Mexico, natural gas from coal, and gas from renewable organic and other unconventional sources. Advancing technology may allow us to draw energy from seawater and from pools of superheated brine.

Another recent technological advancement is the use of nuclear energy to generate electricity. Nuclear power plants are made up of one or more nuclear reactor units. In each unit, uranium undergoes a fission reaction, which produces enormous quantities of heat. During this fission reaction, the nucleus of an atom is split into energized particles called neutrons. The neutrons are released at such great speed that they collide with other atomic nuclei and cause additional splitting action to occur. This chain reaction would be uncontrollable if it did not occur within the walls of the reactor core.

Heat generated by this fission process creates steam from water circulating around the reactor core. Pipes keep the steam under very high pressure and carry it away to the turbine, which drives the electric generator that produces electricity.

Solar energy converts the sun's light into energy that can be used to make electricity. In the near future, the demand for architects that can design buildings to maximize sunlight will grow, as will the demand for installers of solar systems for homes and businesses. According to the American Solar Energy Institute, more than 1.2 million buildings and 250,000 swimming pools in the United States have solar water heating systems.

Wind energy is the fastest growing energy technology in the world for the past three years, according to the American Wind Energy Association. In order to better harness this renewable energy source, engineers will be needed to improve today's windmill design and make them more efficient so that wind energy rates can compete with other available energy sources. Until just a few years ago, most wind farms were concentrated in California, Minnesota, and Iowa, but now wind farm development is present in Colorado, Oregon, Texas, Wisconsin, and Wyoming. According to the America Wind Energy Association, the U.S. wind industry employs over 2,000 people who contribute directly to the economies of 46 states.

U.S. energy consumption is expected to increase at an annual compound rate of about 1 percent between 1997 and 2020. Much of the increased demand will probably be met by imports, with energy imports increasing at an annual compound rate of 2.4 percent, according to the Energy

Information Administration (EIA). (EIA is a statistical agency within the U.S. Department of Energy.) Uncertainties that could affect any predictions include possible interruptions of supply from the Middle East, future decisions by OPEC, U.S. legislation on offshore drilling, increases in energy efficiency by users, changes in technology, and changes in the rate of economic growth and energy consumption.

While the number of oil refineries in the United States is gradually declining, their overall production capacity is increasing due to better efficiency. Much of the oil exploration and refining activity has gone overseas, particularly to offshore Africa, South America, the Middle East, the former Soviet Union, and the North Sea.

Natural gas use is gradually increasing, with some industries switching from coal and oil operations to gas for their power. Production of natural gas sources is expected to rise slightly, according to the U.S. Department of Labor.

Because domestic companies cut way back on exploration and production of oil and gas in the 1980s after worldwide oil prices declined, and because cost-cutting measures were instituted, projections to the year 2008 for engineers do not show an increase. However, the elevated overseas oil production may result in a slight increase in the demand for workers willing to travel.

The energy business is a classic commodity business, complete with extreme market fluctuations. Nevertheless, experts expect that in the long run, oil and gas prices will most likely rise from the historically low levels seen in 1998, stimulating renewed growth in exploration and production.

Job opportunities in the wind energy field will grow significantly, as U.S. wind power capacity will triple or even quadruple in the next decade. Positions that will need to be filled include those of windsmiths, technicians, engineers, avian specialists, electricians, and construction workers. Employers will also need to fill manufacturing, research, development, and management jobs. The American Wind Energy Association estimates that if the United States increases its current wind energy capacity 15-fold, which they do not believe to be unreasonable, our country could stand to gain as many as 150,000 new jobs in that area.

Each article in this book discusses a particular energy occupation in detail. The articles in *Careers in Focus: Energy* appear in Ferguson's *Encyclopedia of Careers and Vocational Guidance* but have been updated and revised with the latest information from the U.S. Department of Labor and other sources. The **Overview** section is a brief introductory description of the duties and responsibilities of a person in the career. Oftentimes, a career may have a variety of job titles. When this is the case, alternative career titles are presented in this section. The **History** section describes the history of the particular job as it relates to the overall development of its industry or field. **The Job** describes the primary and secondary duties of the job. **Requirements** discusses high school and postsecondary education and training requirements, any certification or licensing necessary, and any other personal requirements for success in the job. **Exploring** offers suggestions on how to gain some experience in or knowledge of the particular job before making a firm educational and financial commitment. The focus is on what can be done while still in high school (or in the early years of college) to gain a better understanding of the job. The **Employers** section gives an overview of typical places of employment for the job. **Starting Out** discusses the best ways to land that first job, be it through the college placement office, newspaper ads, or personal contact. The **Advancement** section describes what kind of career path to expect from the job and how to get there. **Earnings** lists salary ranges and describes the typical fringe benefits. The **Work Environment** section describes the typical surroundings and conditions of employment, whether indoors or outdoors, noisy or quiet, social or independent, and so on. Also discussed are typical hours worked, any seasonal fluctuations, and the stresses and strains of the job. The **Outlook** section summarizes the job in terms of the general economy and industry projections. For the most part, Outlook information is obtained from the Bureau of Labor Statistics and is supplemented by information taken from professional associations. Job growth terms follow those used in the *Occupational Outlook Handbook:* Growth described as "much faster than the average" means an increase of 36 percent or more. Growth described as "faster than the average" means an increase of 21 to 35 percent. Growth described as "about as fast as the average" means an increase of 10 to 20 percent. Growth described as "little change or more slowly than the average" means an increase of 0 to 9 percent. "Decline" means a decrease of 1 percent or more. Each article ends with **For More Information,** which lists organizations that can provide career information on training, education, internships, scholarships, and job placement.

Chemical Engineers

	School Subjects
Chemistry	
Physics	
	Personal Skills
Communication/ideas	
Technical/scientific	
	Work Environment
Primarily indoors	
Primarily one location	
	Minimum Education Level
Bachelor's degree	
	Salary Range
$49,418 to $64,760 to $100,000+	
	Certification or Licensing
Recommended	
	Outlook
About as fast as the average	

Overview

Chemical engineers take chemistry out of the laboratory and into the real world. They are involved in evaluating methods and equipment for the mass production of chemicals and other materials requiring chemical processing. They also develop products from these materials, such as plastics, metals, gasoline, detergents, pharmaceuticals, and foodstuffs. They develop or improve safe, environmentally sound processes, determine the least costly production method, and formulate the material for easy use and safe, economic transportation. Approximately 48,000 chemical engineers work in the United States.

History

Chemical engineering, defined in its most general sense as applied chemistry, existed even in early civilizations. Ancient Greeks, for example, distilled alcoholic beverages, as did the Chinese, who by 800 BC had learned to distill alcohol from the fermentation of rice. Aristotle, a fourth-century Greek philosopher, wrote about a process for obtaining fresh water by evaporating and condensing water from the sea.

The foundations of modern chemical engineering were laid out during the Renaissance, when experimentation and the questioning of accepted scientific theories became widespread. This period saw the development of many new chemical processes, such as those for producing sulfuric acid (for fertilizers and textile treatment) and alkalis (for soap). The atomic theories of John Dalton and Amedeo Avogadro, developed in the 1800s, supplied the theoretical underpinning for modern chemistry and chemical engineering.

With the advent of large-scale manufacturing in the mid-19th century, modern chemical engineering began to take shape. Chemical manufacturers were soon required to seek out chemists familiar with manufacturing processes. These early chemical engineers were called chemical technicians or industrial chemists. The first course in chemical engineering was taught in 1888 at the Massachusetts Institute of Technology, and by 1900, the term "chemical engineer" had become a widely used job title.

Chemical engineers are employed in increasing numbers to design new and more efficient ways to produce chemicals and chemical by-products. In the United States, they have been especially important in the development of petroleum-based fuels for automotive vehicles. Their achievements range from the large-scale production of plastics, antibiotics, and synthetic rubbers to the development of high-octane gasoline.

The Job

Chemical engineering is one of the four major engineering disciplines (the others are electrical, mechanical, and civil). Because chemical engineers are rigorously trained not only in chemistry but also in physics, mathematics, and other sciences such as biology or geology, they are among the most versatile of all engineers, with many specialties, and are employed in many industries. Chemical industries, which transform raw materials into desired products, employ the largest number of chemical engineers.

Research engineers work with chemists to develop new processes and products, or they may develop better methods to make existing products. Product ideas may originate with the company's marketing department; with a chemist, chemical engineer, or other specialist; or with a customer. The basic chemical process for the product is then developed in a laboratory, where various experiments are conducted to determine the process's viability. Some projects die here.

Others go on to be developed and refined at pilot plants, which are small-scale versions of commercial plants. Chemical engineers in these plants run tests on the processes and make any necessary modifications. They strive to improve the process, reduce safety hazards and waste, and cut production time and costs. Throughout the development stage, engineers keep detailed records of the proceedings, and they may abandon projects that aren't viable.

When a new process is judged to be viable, *process design engineers* determine how the product can most efficiently be produced on a large scale while still guaranteeing a consistently high quality result. These engineers consider process requirements and cost, convenience and safety for the operators, waste minimization, legal regulations, and preservation of the environment. Besides working on the steps of the process, they also work on the design of the equipment to be used in the process. These chemical engineers are often assisted in plant and equipment design by mechanical, electrical, and civil engineers.

Project engineers oversee the construction of new plants and installation of new equipment. In construction, chemical engineers may work as *field engineers,* who are involved in the testing and initial operation of the equipment and assist in plant start-up and operator training. Once a process is fully implemented at a manufacturing plant, *production engineers* supervise the day-to-day operations. They are responsible for the rate of production, scheduling, worker safety, quality control, and other important operational concerns.

Chemical engineers working in environmental control are involved in waste management, recycling, and control of air and water pollution. They work with the engineers in research and development, process design, equipment and plant construction, and production to incorporate environmental protection measures into all stages of the chemical engineering process.

As *technical sales engineers,* chemical engineers may work with customers of manufactured products to determine what best fits their needs. They answer questions such as "Could our products be used more economically than those now in use? Why does this paint peel?" etc. Others work as managers, making policy and business decisions and overseeing the training of new personnel.

Still others may act as *biomedical engineers* who work with physicians to develop systems to track critical chemical processes in the body or look for the best method of administering a particular drug to a patient. The variety of job descriptions is almost limitless because of chemical engineers' versatility and adaptability.

Requirements

High School

High school students interested in chemical engineering should take all the mathematics and science courses their schools offer. These should include algebra, geometry, calculus, trigonometry, chemistry, physics, and biology. Computer science courses are also highly recommended. In addition, students should take four years of English, and a foreign language is valuable. To enhance their desirability, students should participate in high school science and engineering clubs and other extracurricular activities.

Postsecondary Training

A bachelor's degree in chemical engineering is the minimum educational requirement for entering the field. For some positions, an M.S., an M.B.A., or a Ph.D. may be required. A Ph.D. may be essential for advancement in research, teaching, and administration.

For their college studies, students need a chemical engineering program approved by the Accreditation Board for Engineering and Technology and the American Institute of Chemical Engineers. There are about 145 accredited undergraduate programs in chemical engineering in the United States offering bachelor's degrees. Some engineering programs last five or six years; these often include work experience in industry.

As career plans develop, students should consult with advisors about special career paths in which they are interested. Those who want to teach or conduct research will need a graduate degree. There are approximately 140 accredited chemical engineering graduate programs in the United States. A master's degree generally takes two years of study beyond undergraduate school, while a Ph.D. program requires four to six years.

In graduate school, students specialize in one aspect of chemical engineering, such as chemical kinetics or biotechnology. Graduate education also helps to obtain promotions, and some companies offer tuition reimbursement to encourage employees to take graduate courses. For engineers who would like to become managers, a master's degree in business administration may be helpful. Chemical engineers must be prepared for a lifetime of education to keep up with the rapid advances in technology.

Certification or Licensing

Chemical engineers must be licensed as a professional engineer if they wish to work in the public sector. All 50 states and the District of Columbia have specific licensing requirements, which include graduation from an accredited engineering school, passing a written exam, and having at least four years of engineering experience. About one-third of all chemical engineers are licensed; they are called *registered engineers.*

Other Requirements

Important personal qualities are honesty, accuracy, objectivity, and perseverance. In addition, chemical engineers must be inquisitive, open-minded, creative, and flexible. Problem-solving ability is essential. To remain competitive in the job market, they should display initiative and leadership skills, exhibit the ability to work well in teams and collaborate across disciplines, and be able to work with people of different languages and cultures.

Exploring

High school students should join science clubs and take part in other extracurricular activities and such organizations as the Junior Engineering Technical Society (JETS). JETS participants have opportunities to enter engineering design and problem-solving contests and to learn team development skills. Science contests are also a good way to apply principles learned in classes to a special project. Students can also subscribe to the American Chemical Society's *Chem Matters,* a quarterly magazine for high school chemistry students.

College students can join professional associations, such as the American Chemical Society, the American Institute of Chemical Engineers, and the Society of Manufacturing Engineers (composed of individual associations with specific fields of interest), as student affiliates. Membership benefits include subscription to magazines (some of them geared specifically toward students) that provide the latest industry information. College students can also contact local sections of these associations to arrange to talk with some chemical engineers about what they do. Contacts through professional organizations can also help them find summer or co-op work experiences.

In addition, the Society of Women Engineers has a mentor program in which high school and college women are matched with a society member in their area. This member is available to answer questions and provide a firsthand introduction to a career in engineering.

Employers

There are approximately 48,000 chemical engineers working in the United States. While the majority of chemical engineers (about 70 percent) work in manufacturing industries, others are employed by the federal and state governments, colleges and universities, and research and testing services. The list of individual employers, if cited, would take many pages. However, the following industry classifications indicate where most chemical engineers are employed: fuels, electronics, food and consumer products, design and construction, materials, aerospace, biotechnology, pharmaceuticals, environmental control, pulp and paper, public utilities, and consultation firms. Because of the nature of their training and background, chemical engineers can easily obtain employment with another company in a completely different field if necessary or desired.

Starting Out

Most chemical engineers obtain their first position through company recruiters sent to college campuses. Others may find employment with companies with whom they have had summer or work-study arrangements. Many respond to advertisements in professional journals or newspapers. The Internet now offers multiple opportunities to job seekers, and many libraries have programs that offer assistance in making use of the available job listings. Chemical engineers may also contact colleges and universities regarding positions as part-time teaching or laboratory assistants if they wish to continue study for a graduate degree. Student members of professional societies often use the employment services of these organizations, including resume data banks, online job listings, national employment clearinghouses, and employers' mailing lists.

Typically, new recruits begin as trainees or process engineers. They often begin work under the supervision of seasoned engineers. Many participate in special training programs designed to orient them to company processes, procedures, policies, and products. This allows the company to determine where the new personnel may best fulfill their needs. After this training period, new employees often rotate positions to get an all-around experience in working for the company.

Advancement

Entry-level personnel usually advance to project or production engineers after learning the ropes in product manufacturing. They may then be assigned to sales and marketing. A large percentage of engineers no longer do engineering work by the tenth year of their employment. At that point, they often advance to supervisory or management positions. An M.B.A. enhances their opportunities for promotion. A doctoral degree is essential for university teaching or supervisory research positions. Some engineers may decide at this point that they prefer to start their own consulting firms. Continued advancement, raises, and increased responsibility are not automatic but depend upon sustained demonstration of leadership skills.

Earnings

Chemical engineering is one of the highest paid scientific professions. Salaries vary with education, experience, industry, and employer. A 1999 survey by the National Association of Colleges and Employers found average starting salaries as follows: B.S. $49,418; M.S. $56,100; and Ph.D. $68,491. According to the U.S. Department of Labor, in 1998 the median annual income of chemical engineers was $64,760. The highest paid 10 percent earned over $92,240. For chemical engineers with doctoral degrees and many years of experience who attain supervisory and management positions, salaries above $100,000 are not unusual. The American Institute of Chemical Engineers surveyed its members in 2000 and reports the following 1999 median salaries for its members by industry: federal government, $76,600; education, $80,000; research and development, $72,750; metals and minerals, $67,800; natural gas, $89,000; petrochemicals and petroleum products, $90,000; and pharmaceuticals, $75,500.

Work Environment

Because the industries in which chemical engineers work are so varied—from academia to waste treatment and disposal—the working conditions also vary. Most chemical engineers work in clean, well-maintained offices, laboratories, and plants, although some occasionally work outdoors, particularly construction engineers. Travel to new or existing plants may be required. Some chemical engineers work with dangerous chemicals, but the adoption of safe working practices has greatly reduced potential health hazards. Chemical engineers at institutions of higher learning spend their time in classrooms or research laboratories.

The workweek for a chemical engineer in manufacturing is usually 40 hours, although many work longer hours. Because plants often operate around the clock, they may work different shifts or have irregular hours.

Outlook

The U.S. Department of Labor projects employment for chemical engineers to grow about as fast as the average through 2008. As long as chemical companies research and develop new chemicals and increase the efficiency of their production, there will be openings for chemical engineers. However, graduates may face stiff competition for engineering jobs in manufacturing as the number of these openings is projected to be lower than the number of graduates. Nevertheless, the broad technical base of a chemical engineer's education makes this person an appealing candidate for employment to companies in many related fields.

For More Information

For information on internships, summer jobs, and co-op programs, contact:

American Chemical Society
1155 16th Street, NW
Washington, DC 20036
Tel: 800-227-5558
Web: http://www.acs.org

For information on awards, student chapters, and career opportunities, contact:

American Institute of Chemical Engineers
3 Park Avenue
New York, NY 10016-5991
Tel: 800-242-4363
Email: xpress@aiche.org
Web: http://www.aiche.org

For information about JETS programs, products, and a chemical engineering career brochure, contact:

Junior Engineering Technical Society (JETS)
1420 King Street, Suite 405
Alexandria, VA 22314-2794
Tel: 703-548-5387
Email: jets@nae.edu
Web: http://www.jets.org

For information on training programs, seminars, and how to become a student member, contact:

Society of Manufacturing Engineers
PO Box 930
One SME Drive
Dearborn, MI 48121-0930
Tel: 800-733-4763
Web: http://www.sme.org

For career guidance literature and information on scholarships and mentor programs, contact:

Society of Women Engineers
230 East Ohio Street, Suite 400
Chicago, IL 60611-3265
Tel: 312-596-5223
Email: hq@swe.org
Web: http://www.swe.org

Chemical Technicians

	School Subjects
Chemistry Mathematics	
	Personal Skills
Following instructions Technical/scientific	
	Work Environment
Primarily indoors Primarily one location	
	Minimum Education Level
Some postsecondary training	
	Salary Range
$21,000 to $31,000 to $42,000+	
	Certification or Licensing
None available	
	Outlook
Little change or more slowly than the average	

Overview

Chemical technicians assist chemists and chemical engineers in the research, development, and manufacturing of chemicals and chemical-based products.

History

The practice of chemistry goes back thousands of years to the earliest days when humans extracted medicinal juices from plants and shaped metals into tools and utensils for daily life. In the late 18th century, chemistry became established as a science when Antoine Lavoisier formulated the law of the conservation of matter. From that time until the present, the number and types of products attributed to the development and expansion of chemistry is almost incalculable.

The period following World War I witnessed an enormous expansion of chemical technology and its application to the production of goods and consumer products such as high octane gasoline, antifreeze, pesticides, pharmaceuticals, plastics, and artificial fibers and fabrics. This rapid expansion increased the need for professionally trained chemists and technicians. The technicians, with their basic chemical knowledge and manual skills, were able to handle the tasks that did not require the specialized education of their bosses. These nonprofessionals sometimes had the title of *junior chemist.*

During the last 30 years, however, there has been a radical change in the status of the chemical technician from a "mere" assistant to a core professional. Automation and computerization have increased laboratory efficiency, and corporate downsizing has eliminated many layers of intermediate hierarchy. The result has been to increase the level of responsibility and independence, meaning greater recognition of the importance of today's highly skilled and trained chemical technicians.

The Job

Most chemical technicians who work in the chemical industry are involved in the development, testing, and manufacturing of plastics, paints, detergents, synthetic fibers, industrial chemicals, and pharmaceuticals. Others work in the petroleum, aerospace, metals, electronics, automotive, and construction industries. Some chemical technicians work in universities and government laboratories.

They may work in any of the fields of chemistry, such as analytical, biochemistry, inorganic, organic, physical, or any of the many subbranches of chemistry. Chemical engineering, which is a combination of chemistry and engineering, develops or improves manufacturing processes for making commercial amounts of chemicals, many of which were previously produced only in small quantities in laboratory glassware or a pilot plant.

Within these subfields, chemical technicians work in research and development, design and production, and quality control. In research and development, *chemical laboratory technicians* often work with Ph.D. chemists and chemical engineers to set up and monitor laboratory equipment and instruments, prepare laboratory setups, and record data.

Technicians often determine the chemical composition, concentration, stability, and level of purity on a wide range of materials. These may include ores, minerals, pollutants, foods, drugs, plastics, dyes, paints, detergents, chemicals, paper, and petroleum products. Although chemists or chemical engineers may design an experiment, technicians help them create process designs, develop written procedures, and devise computer simulations. They also select all necessary glassware, reagents, chemicals, and equipment. Technicians also perform analyses and report test results.

In the design and production area, chemical technicians work closely with chemical engineers to monitor the large-scale production of compounds and to help develop and improve the processes and equipment used. They prepare tables, charts, sketches, diagrams, and flowcharts that record and summarize the collected data.

They work with pipelines, valves, pumps, and metal and glass tanks. Chemical technicians often use their input to answer manufacturing questions, such as how to transfer materials from one point to another, and to build, install, modify, and maintain processing equipment. They also train and supervise production operators. They may operate small-scale equipment for determining process parameters.

Fuel technicians determine viscosities of oils and fuels, measure flash points (the temperature at which fuels catch fire), pour points (the coldest temperature at which the fuel can flow), and the heat output of fuels.

Pilot plant operators make erosion and corrosion tests on new construction materials to determine their suitability. They prepare chemicals for field testing and report on the effectiveness of new design concepts.

Applied research technicians help design new manufacturing or research equipment.

Requirements

High School

Several years of science and mathematics should be taken in high school, and computer training is also important. While a minority of employers still hire high school graduates and place them into their own training programs, the majority prefer to hire graduates of community colleges who have completed two-year chemical technician programs or even bachelor degree recipients. If a four-year college enrollment is planned, as much as three years of high school mathematics, including algebra, geometry, and trigonometry; three years of physical sciences, including chemistry; and four years of English should be studied.

Postsecondary Training

Graduates of community college programs are productive much sooner than untrained individuals because they have the technical knowledge, laboratory experience, and skills for the job. Computer courses are necessary as computers and computer-interfaced equipment are routinely used in the field. Realizing that many students become aware of technical career possibilities too late to satisfy college requirements, many community and technical colleges that offer chemical technician programs may also have noncredit courses that allow students to meet college entrance requirements.

Approximately 40 two-year colleges in the United States have chemical technology programs. Once enrolled in a two-year college program designed for chemical technicians, students should expect to take a number of chemistry courses with strong emphasis on laboratory work and the presentation of data. These courses include basic concepts of modern chemistry, such as atomic structure, descriptive chemistry of both organic and inorganic substances, analytical methods including quantitative and instrumental analysis, and physical properties of substances. Other courses include communications, physics, mathematics, industrial safety, and organic laboratory equipment and procedures.

Other Requirements

Besides the educational requirements, certain personal characteristics are necessary for successful chemical technicians. They must have both the ability and the desire to use mental and manual skills. They should also have a good supply of patience because experiments must frequently be repeated several times. They should be precise and like doing detailed work. Mechanical aptitude and good powers of observation are also needed. They should be able to follow directions closely and enjoy solving problems. Chemical technicians also need excellent organizational and communication skills. Other important qualities are a desire to learn new skills and a willingness to accept responsibility. In addition, technicians should have good eyesight, color perception, and hand-eye coordination.

Exploring

Students should join their high school science clubs or organizations, as well as take part in extracurricular activities such as the Junior Engineering Technical Society (JETS). Science contests are a good way to apply principles learned in classes to a special project. JETS offers interested students opportunities to compete in engineering and design teams. Check out its Web site, www.jets.org, for more information. Students can also subscribe to the American Chemical Society's *Chem Matters,* a quarterly magazine for students taking chemistry in high school. Examples of topics covered in the magazine include the chemistry of lipstick, suntan products, contact lenses, and carbon-14 dating. Also, qualifying students can participate in Project SEED (Summer Education Experience for the Disadvantaged), a summer program designed to provide high school students from economically disadvantaged homes the opportunity to experience science research in a laboratory environment.

College students can become student affiliates of professional associations such as the American Chemical Society and the American Institute of Chemical Engineers. Membership allows students to experience the professionalism of a career in chemistry. They can also contact local sections of these organizations to talk with chemists and chemical engineers about what they do. Contacts from professional associations can also help them find summer or co-op work experiences. All these opportunities can help individuals determine if a career in chemistry is a good choice.

Employers

Almost all chemical laboratories, no matter their size or function, employ chemical technicians to assist their chemists or chemical engineers with research as well as routine laboratory work. Therefore, chemical technicians can find employment wherever chemistry is involved: in industrial laboratories, government agencies such as the Departments of Health and Agriculture, and at colleges and universities. They can work in almost any field of chemical activity, such as industrial manufacturing of all kinds, pharmaceuticals, food, and production of chemicals.

Starting Out

Graduates of chemical technology programs often find jobs during the last term of their two-year programs. Some companies work with local community colleges and technical schools to maintain a supply of trained chemical technicians. Recruiters regularly visit most colleges where chemical technology programs are offered. Most employers recruit locally or regionally. Because companies hire locally and work closely with technical schools, placement offices are usually successful in finding jobs for their graduates.

Some recruiters also go to four-year colleges and look for chemists with bachelor's degrees. Whether a company hires bachelor's-level chemists or two-year chemical technology graduates depends upon both the outlook of the company and the local supply of graduates.

Internships and co-op work are highly regarded by employers, and participation in such programs is a good way to get a foot in the door. Many two- and four-year schools have co-op programs in which full-time students work about 20 hours a week for a local company. Such programs may be available to high school seniors as well. Students in these programs develop a good knowledge of the employment possibilities and frequently stay with their co-op employers.

More and more companies are using contract workers to perform technicians' jobs, and this is another way to enter the field. There are local agencies that place technicians with companies for special projects or temporary assignments that last anywhere from a month to a year or more. Many of these contract workers are later hired on a full-time basis.

Advancement

Competent chemical technicians can expect to have long-term career paths. Top research and development positions are open to technically trained people, whether they start out with an associate's degree in chemical technology, a bachelor's degree in chemistry, or just a lot of valuable experience with no degree. There are also opportunities for advancement in the areas of technology development and technology management, providing comparable pay for these separate but equal paths. Some companies have the same career path for all technicians, regardless of education level. Other companies have different career ladders for technicians and chemists but will promote qualified technicians to chemists and move them up that path. Advancement opportunities at Fortune 500 companies are particularly plentiful.

Some companies may require additional formal schooling for promotion, and the associate's degree can be a stepping-stone toward a bachelor's degree in chemistry. Many companies encourage their technicians to continue their education, and most reimburse tuition costs. Continuing education in the form of seminars, workshops, and in-company presentations is also important for advancement. Chemical technicians who want to advance must keep up with current developments in the field by reading trade and technical journals and publications.

Earnings

The median salary in 1998 for all science technicians and technologists was $31,000 according to the Bureau of Labor Statistics. Ten percent earned less than $21,000 and 10 percent earned over $42,000. The median earnings for chemical technicians working in research and testing were $24,000. Those who worked in drug manufacturing earned $32,000. Salaries are highest in private industry and lowest in colleges and universities. Salaries vary by the education, experience, and responsibility level of technicians as well as the type and size of the company where they are employed. The greatest variation in salary is from region to region. Starting salaries are highest in the Middle Atlantic region and lowest in the East South Central region. If technicians belong to a union, wages and benefits depend on the union agreement. However, the percentage of technicians who belong to a union is very small. Benefits depend on the employer, but they usually include paid vacations and holidays, insurance, and tuition refund plans. Technicians normally work a five-day, 40-hour week. Occasional overtime may be necessary.

Work Environment

The chemical industry is one of the safest industries in which to work. Laboratories and plants normally have safety committees and safety engineers who closely monitor equipment and practices to minimize hazards. Chemical technicians usually receive safety training both in school and at work to recognize potential hazards and to take appropriate measures.

Most chemical laboratories are clean and well lighted. Chemical technicians usually have very few people working in the immediate area. Technicians often work at tables and benches while operating laboratory equipment and are usually provided office or desk space to record data and prepare reports. The work can sometimes be monotonous and repetitive, as when making samples or doing repetitive testing. Chemical plants are usually clean, and the number of operating personnel for the space involved is often very low.

Outlook

Employment of science technicians will increase more slowly than the average through 2008, according to the *Occupational Outlook Handbook*. Employment prospects are better in specialty chemicals and parts of the industry that sell directly to consumers, such as pharmaceutical firms. Technologies expected to grow include biotechnology, environment, catalysis, materials science, communication and computer technology, and energy. Business areas with the most potential for growth include environmental services and "earth-friendly" products, analytical development and services, custom or niche products and services, and quality control. Growth, however, will be offset by a general slowdown in overall employment in the chemical industry.

Graduates of chemical technology programs will continue to face competition from bachelor's level chemists. The chemical and chemical-related industries will continue to become increasingly sophisticated in both their products and their manufacturing techniques. Automation, new products, and complex production methods assure the demand for trained technicians.

For More Information

For general career information, as well as listings of chemical technology programs, internships, and summer job opportunities, contact:

American Chemical Society
1155 16th Street, NW
Washington, DC 20036
Tel: 800-227-5558
Web: http://www.acs.org

For information on awards, student chapters, and career opportunities, contact:

American Institute of Chemical Engineers
3 Park Avenue
New York, NY 10016-5991
Tel: 800-242-4363
Email: xpress@aiche.org
Web: http://www.aiche.org

For information about JETS programs, products, and a chemical engineering career brochure, contact:

Junior Engineering Technical Society (JETS)
1420 King Street, Suite 405
Alexandria, VA 22314-2794
Tel: 703-548-5387
Email: jets@nae.edu
Web: http://www.jets.org

Chemists

Chemistry Mathematics	School Subjects
Communication/ideas Technical/scientific	Personal Skills
Primarily indoors Primarily one location	Work Environment
Bachelor's degree	Minimum Education Level
$29,500 to $50,100 to $86,260+	Salary Range
None available	Certification or Licensing
About as fast as the average	Outlook

Overview

Chemists are scientists who study the composition, changes, reactions, and transformations of matter. They may specialize in analytical, biological, inorganic, organic, or physical chemistry. They may work in laboratories, hospitals, private companies, government agencies, or colleges and universities. Approximately 96,000 chemists are employed in the United States.

History

About 2,000 years ago, the Egyptians began gathering knowledge about matter and organizing it into systems. This was the beginning of chemistry. They developed what is now known as alchemy, which mixed science with superstition. Alchemists concentrated their efforts on trying to convert lead and other common metals into gold. Alchemy dominated the European chemical scene until modern chemistry started to replace it in the 18th century.

In the late 1700s, Antoine Lavoisier discovered that the weight of the products of a chemical reaction always equaled the combined weight of the original reactants. This discovery became known as the law of the conservation of matter. In the 1800s, the work of scientists such as John Dalton, Humphrey Davy, Michael Faraday, Amadeo Avogadro, Dmitri Mendeleyev, and Julius Meyer laid the foundations for modern chemistry. The latter two men independently established the periodic law and periodic table of elements, making chemistry a rational, predictable science. The technological advances of the Industrial Revolution provided both the necessity and the incentive to get rid of alchemy and make chemistry the science it is today.

The Job

Many chemists work in research and development laboratories. However, some chemists spend most of their time in offices or libraries where they do academic research on new developments or write reports on research results. Often these chemists determine the need for certain products and tell the researchers what experiments or studies to pursue in the laboratory.

Chemists who work in research are usually focused on either basic or applied research. Chemists involved in basic research search for new knowledge about chemicals and chemical properties. This helps scientists broaden their understanding of the chemical world, and often these new discoveries appear later as applied research. Chemists working in applied research use knowledge obtained from basic research to create new and/or better products that may be used by consumers or in manufacturing processes, such as the development of new pharmaceuticals for the treatment of a specific disease or superior plastics for space travel. In addition they may hold marketing or sales positions, advising customers about how to use certain products. These jobs are especially important in the field of agriculture where customers need to know the safe and effective doses of pesticides to use to protect workers, consumers, and the environment.

Chemists who work in marketing and sales must understand the scientific terminology involved so they can translate it into nontechnical terms for the customer.

Some chemists work in quality control and production in manufacturing plants. They work with plant engineers to establish manufacturing processes for specific products and to ensure that the chemicals are safely and effectively handled within the plant.

Chemists also work as instructors in high schools, colleges, and universities. Many at the university level are also involved in basic or applied research. In fact, most of America's basic research is conducted in a university setting.

There are many branches of chemistry, each with a different set of requirements. A chemist may go into basic or applied research, marketing, teaching, or a variety of other related positions. *Analytical chemists* study the composition and nature of rocks, soils, and other substances and develop procedures for analyzing them. They also identify the presence of pollutants in soil, water, and air. *Biological chemists,* also known as *biochemists,* study the composition and actions of complex chemicals in living organisms. They identify and analyze the chemical processes related to biological functions, such as metabolism or reproduction, and are often involved directly in genetics studies. They are also employed in the pharmaceutical and food industries.

The distinction between organic and inorganic chemistry is based upon carbon-hydrogen compounds. Ninety-nine percent of all chemicals that occur naturally contain carbon. *Organic chemists* study the chemical compounds that contain carbon and hydrogen, while *inorganic chemists* study all other substances. *Physical chemists* study the physical characteristics of atoms and molecules. A physical chemist working in a nuclear power plant, for example, may study the properties of the radioactive materials involved in the production of electricity derived from nuclear fission reactions.

Because chemistry is such a diverse field, central to every reaction and the transformation of all matter, it is necessary for chemists to specialize in specific areas. Still, each field covers a wide range of work and presents almost limitless possibilities for experimentation and study. Often, chemists will team up with colleagues in other specialties to seek solutions to their common problems.

Requirements

High School

Students interested in chemistry careers can begin to prepare themselves in high school by taking advanced-level courses in the physical sciences, mathematics, and English. A year each of physics, chemistry, and biology is essential, as are the abilities to read graphs and charts, perform difficult mathematical calculations, and write scientific reports.

Postsecondary Training

The minimum educational requirement for a chemist is a bachelor's degree in science. However, in the upper levels of basic and applied research, and especially in a university setting, most positions are filled by people with doctoral degrees.

Over 600 bachelor's degree programs are accredited by the American Chemical Society. Many colleges and universities also offer advanced degree programs in chemistry. Upon entering college, students majoring in chemistry must expect to take classes in several branches of the field, such as organic, inorganic, analytical, physical chemistry, and biochemistry. Chemistry majors must advance their skills in mathematics, physics, and biology and be proficient with computers.

Other Requirements

Chemists must be detail-oriented, precise workers. They often work with minute quantities, taking minute measurements. They must record all details and reaction changes that may seem insignificant and unimportant to the untrained observer. They must keep careful records of their work and have the patience to repeat experiments over and over again, perhaps varying the conditions in only a small way each time. They should be inquisitive and have an interest in what makes things work and how things fit together. Chemists may work alone or in groups. A successful chemist is not only self-motivated but should be a team player and have good written and oral communication skills.

Exploring

The best means of exploring a career in chemistry while still in high school is to pay attention and work hard in chemistry class. This will give you the opportunity to learn the scientific method, perform chemical experiments, and become familiar with chemical terminology. Contact the department of chemistry at a local college or university to discuss the field and arrange tours of their laboratories or classrooms. Due to the extensive training involved, it is very unlikely that a high school student will be able to get a summer job or internship working in a laboratory. However, you may want to contact local manufacturers or research institutions to explore the possibility.

Employers

Nearly half of the approximately 96,000 chemists employed in the United States work for manufacturing companies. Most of these companies are involved in chemical manufacturing, producing such products as plastics, soaps, paints, drugs, and synthetic materials. Chemists are also needed in industrial manufacturing and pilot plant locations. Examples of large companies that employ many chemists are Dow Chemical, DuPont, Monsanto, Standard Oil, and Campbell Soup.

Chemists also work in government laboratories, such as at the Departments of Health and Agriculture, the Bureau of Standards, and the Bureau of Mines. Chemists may find positions in laboratories at institutions of higher learning that are devoted to research. In addition, some chemists work in full-time teaching positions in high schools and universities.

Starting Out

Once you have a degree in chemistry, job opportunities will begin to open up. Summer jobs may become available after your sophomore or junior year of college. You can attend chemical trade fairs and science and engineering fairs to meet and perhaps interview prospective employers. Professors or faculty advisors may know of job openings, and you can begin breaking into the field by using these connections.

If you are a senior and are interested in pursuing an academic career at a college or university, you should apply to graduate schools. You will want to begin focusing even more on the specific type of chemistry you wish to practice and teach, for example, inorganic chemistry or analytical chemistry. Look for universities that have strong programs and eminent professors in your intended field of specialty. By getting involved with the basic research of a specific branch of chemistry while in graduate school, you can become a highly employable expert in your field.

Advancement

In nonacademic careers, advancement usually takes the form of increased job responsibilities accompanied by salary increases. For example, a chemist may rise from doing basic research in a laboratory to being a group leader, overseeing and directing the work of others. Some chemists eventually leave the laboratory and set up their own consulting businesses, serving the needs of private manufacturing companies or government agencies. Others may accept university faculty positions.

Chemists who work in a university setting follow the advancement procedures for that institution. Typically, a chemist in academia with a doctoral degree will go from instructor to assistant professor to associate professor and finally to full professor. In order to advance through these ranks, faculty members at most colleges and universities are expected to perform original research and publish their papers in scientific journals of chemistry and/or other sciences. As the rank of faculty members increases, so do their duties, salaries, responsibilities, and reputations.

Earnings

Salary levels for chemists vary based on education, experience, and the area in which they work. According to a 1998 survey by the American Chemical Society, the average starting salary for inexperienced chemists with bachelor's degrees was $29,500; for those with master's degrees, it was $38,500; and for those with doctoral degrees, it was $59,300. The Society also reported that a 1999 survey of its members found the median salary for those with a bachelor's degree to be $50,100 per year. The median for its members with a master's was $61,000 and for those with a doctorate, $76,000. The U.S. Department of Labor reported that in 1999 chemists in nonsupervisory, supervisory, and managerial positions with the federal government earned an average of $64,200 annually. The department also found that the highest paid 10 percent of all chemists averaged $86,260 or more per year in 1998.

As highly trained, full-time professionals, most chemists receive health insurance, paid vacations, and sick leave. The specifics of these benefits vary from employer to employer. Chemists who teach at the college or university level usually work on an academic calendar, which means they get extensive breaks from teaching classes during summer and winter recesses.

Work Environment

Most chemists work in clean, well-lighted laboratories that are well organized and neatly kept. They may have their own offices and share laboratory space with other chemists. Some chemists work at such locations as oil wells or refineries, where their working conditions may be uncomfortable. Occasionally, chemical reactions or substances being tested may have strong odors. Other chemicals may be extremely dangerous to the touch, and chemists will have to wear protective devices such as goggles, gloves, and protective clothing and work in special, well-ventilated hoods.

Outlook

The U.S. Department of Labor predicts the employment of chemists to grow at about as fast as the average rate through 2008. The outlook is expected to be particularly good for researchers interested in working in pharmaceutical firms, biotechnology firms, and firms producing specialty chemicals. However, growth is expected to decrease in the industrial chemical and oil industries. Chemists who specialize in polymers, product syntheses, analytical chemistry, and food chemistry should have good opportunities. Aspiring chemists would do well to get doctoral degrees to maximize their opportunities for employment and advancement.

Those wishing to teach at the university or college level should find opportunities but also stiff competition. Although the U.S. Department of Labor projects enrollment in colleges and universities to increase through 2008, many such institutions are choosing to hire adjunct faculty instead of individuals working in full-time, tenure-track positions. Nevertheless, a well-trained chemist should have little trouble finding some type of employment.

For More Information

For a brochure on clinical laboratory careers and other information, contact:

American Association for Clinical Chemistry
2101 L Street, NW, Suite 202
Washington, DC 20037-1558
Tel: 800-892-1400
Web: http://www.aacc.org

For general information about chemistry careers and approved education programs, contact:

American Chemical Society
1155 16th Street, NW
Washington, DC 20036
Tel: 800-227-5558
Web: http://www.acs.org

For fun and educational information on the field of chemistry, check out the following Web site:

Chem 4 Kids
Web: http://www.chem4kids.com

Coal Miners

	School Subjects
Chemistry Earth science	
	Personal Skills
Mechanical/manipulative Technical/scientific	
	Work Environment
Primarily outdoors Primarily one location	
	Minimum Education Level
High school diploma	
	Salary Range
$21,710 to $31,640 to $60,000	
	Certification or Licensing
Required by certain states	
	Outlook
Decline	

Overview

Coal miners extract coal from surface mines and underground mines. To do this, they operate complex and expensive machinery that drills, cuts, scrapes, or shovels earth and coal so that the fuel can be collected. Since coal is hard to reach, large portions of earth must be removed from the surface or dug out of mines so the coal miners can get to it. Some coal miners are explosives experts who use dynamite and other substances to remove earth and make the coal accessible. There are approximately 92,000 coal mining workers employed in the United States.

History

Even before the development of agriculture and weaving, Stone Age people mined for minerals buried in the earth: flints for weaponry, mineral pigments for picture and body painting, and precious metals and stones for ornamentation. Early miners carved out open pits to reach the more accessible materials. Then they dug primitive tunnels underground, using sticks and bones to remove soft or broken rocks. As time went on, early miners learned to break hard rocks by driving metal or wooden wedges into cracks in the surface. An early method for dealing with particularly large, stubborn rocks was to build fires alongside them until they became thoroughly heated and then to dash cold water against them. The sudden contraction would cause the rocks to fracture.

No one knows when coal was first discovered and used for fuel; even ancient peoples in several areas of the globe seem to have known about it. There is evidence that coal was burned in Wales during the Bronze Age about three to four thousand years ago, and by the early Romans in Britain. The first industrial use of coal was in the Middle Ages in England, and the English were far more advanced in mining methods than other nations for many years.

The earliest method of coal production was strip mining, which involves gathering deposits near the earth's surface. Early strip mining did not produce large amounts of coal, because methods of removing soil that lay over the coal were crude and slow. Beginning in 1910, this type of mining became more practical as powered machinery came into use.

Commercial mining started in the United States around 1750, near Richmond, Virginia, with the first recorded commercial shipment of American coal: 32 tons from Virginia to New York. Most of the coal produced was used to manufacture shells and shot for the Revolutionary War.

The coal industry played a vital role in the rapid industrial development of the United States. Its importance increased dramatically during the 1870s as the railroads expanded and the steel industry developed, and during the 1880s when steam was first used to generate electric power. The production of bituminous coal doubled each decade from 1880 to 1910, and by 1919 production was more than 500 million tons.

Coal is the country's primary source of energy. Its use declined after World War II, when natural gas and oil became economically competitive. Rising prices and worries about the availability of oil have made coal a major energy source again. Coal production in the United States reached one billion tons for the first time in 1990. Today about half of the nation's electricity is generated by burning coal.

Modern technology and improved management have revolutionized coal mining in the last century. Specialized machinery has been developed that replaces human effort with electric, pneumatic, hydraulic, and mechanical power, which are remotely controlled in some applications by computers. This means that highly skilled technicians and workers are needed to direct, operate, maintain, modify, and control the work performed by very expensive machinery.

The Job

Coal miners work in two kinds of coal mines: surface and underground. The mining method used is determined by the depth and location of the coal seam and the geological formations around it. In surface or strip mining, the overburden—the earth above the coal seam—has to be removed before the coal can be dug out. Then, after the mining has been completed, the overburden is replaced so the land can be reclaimed. For underground mining, entries and tunnels are constructed so that workers and equipment can reach the coal.

The machinery used in coal mining is extremely complex and expensive. There are power shovels that can move 3,500 tons of earth in an hour and continuous mining machines that can rip 12 tons of coal from an underground seam in a minute. Longwall shearers can extract the coal at an even faster rate. The job of coal miners is to operate these machines safely and efficiently. Their specific duties depend on the type of mine that employs them and the machinery they operate.

Drillers operate drilling machines to bore holes in the overburden at points selected by the blasters. They must be careful that the drill doesn't bind or stop while in operation. They may replace worn or broken drill parts using hand tools, change drill bits, and lubricate the equipment.

Stripping shovel operators and *dragline operators* control the shovels and draglines that scoop up and move the broken overburden, which is pushed within their reach by the bulldozers. With the overburden removed, the coal is exposed so that machines with smaller shovels can remove it from the seam and load it into trucks.

Underground mining uses three methods to extract the coal that lies deep beneath the surface. These methods are continuous, longwall, and conventional mining.

Continuous mining is the most widely used method of mining underground coal. It is a system that uses a hydraulically operated machine that mines and loads coal in one step. Cutting wheels attached to hydraulic lifts rip coal from the seam. Then mechanical arms gather the coal from the tunnel floor and dump it onto a conveyor, which moves the coal to a shuttle car or another conveyor belt to be carried out of the mine. *Continuous-mining machine operators* sit or lie in the cab of the machine or operate it remotely. Either way, they move the machine into the mining area and manipulate levers to position the cutting wheels against the coal. They and their helpers may adjust, repair, and lubricate the machine and change cutting teeth.

In longwall mining, coal is also cut and loaded in one operation. With steel canopies supporting the roof above the work area, the mining machinery moves along a wall while its plow blade or cutting wheel shears the coal from the seam and automatically loads it onto a conveyor belt for transportation out of the mine. *Longwall-mining machine operators* advance the cutting device either manually or by remote control. They monitor lights and gauges on the control panel and listen for unusual sounds that signal or indicate a malfunction in the equipment. As the wall in front of the longwall mining machine is cut away, the operator and face personnel move the roof supports forward, allowing the roof behind the supports to cave in.

Conventional mining, unlike continuous or longwall mining, is done in separate steps: first the coal is blasted from the seam, then it is picked up and loaded. Of the three underground methods, conventional mining requires the largest number of workers. *Cutter operators* work a self-propelled machine equipped with a circular, toothed chain that travels around a blade six to 15 feet long. They drive the machine into the working area and saw a channel along the bottom and sides of the coal face, a procedure that makes the blasting more effective because it relieves some of the pressure caused by the explosion. Cutter operators may also adjust and repair the machine, replace dull teeth, and shovel debris from the channel. Using mobile machines, *drilling-machine operators* bore blast holes in the coal face after first determining the depth of the undercut and where to place the holes. Then *blasters* place explosive charges in the holes and detonate them to shatter the coal. After the blast, *loading-machine operators* drive electric loading machines to the area and manipulate the levers that control the mechanical arms to gather up the loose coal and load it onto shuttle cars or conveyors to be carried out of the mine.

Coal mining technicians play an important role in the mining process. By the time the mining actually starts, coal mining technicians have already helped the managers, engineers, and scientists to survey, test drill, and analyze the coal deposit for depth and quality. They have also mapped the surface and helped plan the drilling and blasting to break up the rock and soil that cover the coal. The technicians have also helped prepare permits that must be filed with federal and state governments before mining can begin. Information must be provided on how the land will be mined and reclaimed; its soil, water conditions, and vegetation; wildlife conservation; and how archaeological resources will be protected.

The coal mining technicians also assist the mining engineers and superintendents in selecting the machinery used in mining. Such a plan must include selecting machines of a correct size and capacity to match other machinery and planning the sequences for efficient use of machines. The plan also includes mapping roads out of the mine pit, planning machine and road maintenance and, above all, using safety methods for the entire operation.

Ventilation technicians operate dust counting, gas quantity, and air volume measuring instruments. They record or plot this data and plan or assist in planning the direction of air flow through mine workings. Ventilation technicians also help prescribe the fan installations required to accomplish the desired air flow.

Geological aides gather geological data as mining activities progress. They identify rocks and minerals; record and map structural changes; locate drill holes; and identify rocks, coal, and minerals in drill cores. They also map geological information from drill core data, gather samples, and map results on mine plans.

Chemical analysts analyze mine, mill, and coal samples by using volumetric or instrumental methods of analysis. They also write reports on the findings.

Mining work is hard, dirty, and often dangerous. Workers are often characterized by the concern they have for their fellow miners. There is no room for carelessness in this occupation. The safety of all workers depends on teamwork, with everyone alert and careful to avoid accidents.

Requirements

High School

A high school diploma is a minimum educational requirement. Coal miners must be at least 18 years of age and in good physical condition to withstand the rigors of the work.

To work in this field, you should complete at least two years of mathematics, including algebra and geometry, and four years of English and language skills courses, with emphasis on reading, writing, and communication training.

You should also take physics and chemistry. Computer skills are also important, particularly knowledge of computer-aided drafting and design programs. Courses in mechanical drawing or drafting are also helpful.

Postsecondary Training

Federal laws require that all mine workers be given safety and health training before starting work and be retrained annually thereafter. Federal and state laws also require preservice training and annual retraining in subjects such as health and safety regulations and first aid.

It is possible to start a coal mining career as an unskilled worker with a high school diploma. But it is difficult to advance within the coal mining industry without the foundation skills. In general, companies prefer employees who bring formally acquired technical knowledge and skills to the job.

The first year of study in a typical two-year coal mining technician program in a technical or community college includes courses in the basics of coal mining, applied mathematics, mining law, coal mining ventilation and atmospheric control, communication skills, technical reporting, fundamentals of electricity, mining machinery, physical geology, surveying and graphics, mine safety and accident prevention, roof and rib control, and industrial economics and financing.

The second year includes courses in mine instrumentation and electrical systems, electrical maintenance, hydraulic machinery, machine transmissions and drive trains, basic welding, coal mine environmental impacts and control, coal and coal mine atmosphere sampling and analysis, mine machinery and systems automation and control, application of computers to coal mining operations, and first aid and mine rescue.

In some programs, students spend the summer working as interns at coal mining companies. Internships provide a clear picture of the field and help you choose the work area that best fits your abilities. You will gain experience using charts, graphs, blueprints, maps, and machinery and develop confidence through an approach to the real operation of the industry.

Certification or Licensing

Requirements for certification of mine workers vary. A state may require that any person engaged at the face of the mine first obtain a certificate of competency as a miner from the state's miner's examining board. In some cases, a miner may obtain a certificate of competency after completing one year of underground work. A miner who has an associate's degree in coal mine technology may be able to obtain the certificate after completing six months of underground work.

For those seeking a certificate of competency as a mine examiner or manager, a state may require at least four years of underground experience; graduates with associate's degrees in coal mining technology, however, may be able to qualify after only three years of experience.

Coal mining technician students can usually meet the state's criteria for employment while still in their technician preparatory program. It is important to be familiar with these criteria if technicians plan to work in a state other than the one where they begin their education and work experience.

Other Requirements

To be a successful coal miner, you will need to work well with others and accept supervision. You must also learn to work independently and accept responsibility. You must be accurate and careful as mistakes can be expensive and hazardous, even fatal.

The union to which most unionized coal miners belong is the United Mine Workers of America, although some are covered by the Southern Labor Union, the Progressive Mine Workers, or the International Union of Operating Engineers. Some independent unions also operate within single firms.

Exploring

Because of the age limitation for coal miners, opportunities do not exist for most high school students to gain actual experience. If you are over the age of 18, you may be able to find summer work as a laborer in a coal mine, performing routine tasks that require no previous experience. Older students may also investigate the possibility of summer or part-time employment in metal mines, quarries, oil drilling operations, heavy construction, road building, or truck driving. While this work may not be directly related to your career goals, the aptitudes required for the jobs are similar to those needed in mining, and the experience may prove useful.

Employers

In 1998, there were about 251,000 wage and salary jobs in mining and quarrying, about 92,000 of them in coal mining. Most coal miners work in private industry for mining companies. Some opportunities also exist with federal and state governments.

Starting Out

The usual method of entering this field is by direct application to the employment offices of the individual coal mining companies. However, mining machine operators must "come up through the ranks," acquiring the necessary skills on the job.

New employees start as trainees, or "red hats." After the initial training period, they work at routine tasks that do not require much skill, such as shoveling coal onto conveyors. As they gain more experience and become familiar with the mining operations, they are put to work as helpers to experienced machine operators. In this way they eventually learn how to operate the machines themselves.

Coal mining technicians are usually hired by recruiters from major employers before completing their last year of technical school. Industry recruiters regularly visit the campuses of schools with coal mining technician programs and work with the schools' placement officers.

Many two-year graduates take jobs emphasizing basic operational functions. Technicians are then in a position to compete for higher positions, in most cases through the system of job bidding, which considers such factors as formal education, experience, and seniority.

In union mines, when a vacancy occurs and a machine operator job is available, an announcement is posted so that any qualified employee can apply for the position. In most cases the job is given to the person with the most seniority.

Advancement

Advancement opportunities for coal miners are limited. The usual progression is from trainee to general laborer to machine operator's helper. After acquiring the skills needed to operate the machinery, helpers may apply for machine operator jobs as they become available. All qualified workers, however, compete for those positions, and vacancies are almost always filled by workers with the most seniority. A few coal miners become supervisors, but additional training is required for supervisory and management jobs.

After a period of on-the-job experience, coal mining technicians may become supervisors, sales representatives, or possibly even private consultants or special service contractors.

Technical sales representatives work for manufacturers of mining equipment and supplies and sell such products as explosives, flotation chemicals, rock drills, hoists, crushers, grinding mills, classifiers, materials handling equipment, and safety equipment.

Earnings

According to the National Mining Association, the average miner's salary in the United States is $49,000 per year. The U.S. Department of Labor reports that mining machine operators earned a median annual salary of $31,640 in 1998. The lowest paid 10 percent earned less than $21,710. Coal miners with considerable experience may earn more than $60,000 annually.

Among coal miners, earnings vary according to experience and type of mine. Highest paid are seasoned workers in deep underground mines. Coal miners at strip and auger mines are paid slightly less. At the low end, utility workers and unskilled laborers at coal preparation plants earn the least.

These figures do not include overtime or incentive pay. Miners get time and a half or double time for overtime hours. Coal miners who work evening and night shifts typically receive slightly higher wages.

Most coal miners also receive health and life insurance, as well as pension benefits. The insurance generally includes hospitalization, surgery, convalescent care, rehabilitation services, and maternity benefits for the workers and their dependents. The pension size depends on the worker's age at retirement and the number of years of service. In addition, most mine workers are given 10 holidays a year as well as vacation days earned according to length of service.

Work Environment

Coal mining is hard work involving harsh and sometimes hazardous conditions. Workers in surface mines are outdoors in all kinds of weather, while those underground work in tunnels that are cramped, dark, dusty, wet, and cold. They are all subjected to loud noise from the machinery and work that is physically demanding and dirty.

Since passage of the Coal Mine Health and Safety Act in 1969, mine operators have improved the ventilation and lighting in underground mines and have taken steps to eliminate safety hazards for workers. Nevertheless, operators of the heavy machinery both on the surface and below ground run the risk of injury or death from accidents. Other possible hazards for underground miners include roof falls and cave-ins, poisonous and explosive gases, and long exposure to coal dust. After a number of years, workers may develop pneumoconiosis, or "black lung," which is a disabling and sometimes fatal disease.

Outlook

Employment in mining is expected to decline by about 23 percent through 2008. Technological advances have increased productivity but reduced the number of workers in the field. Stricter federal environmental regulations, such as the 1990 Clean Air Act Amendments, and increased foreign competition will limit growth in this industry.

In response to the energy crisis in California, the Bush administration has proposed the construction of new coal-powered electric plants as well as the development of clean-coal technologies for existing coal-powered plants. If these proposals are implemented, coal miners and other workers in the industry may enjoy improved employment opportunities.

Coal is mined in 25 states. Three states—Kentucky, Wyoming, and West Virginia—account for over half of all U.S. coal production. Other states with strong employment include Alabama, Illinois, Ohio, Pennsylvania, and Virginia. Because coal is a major resource for the production of such products as steel and cement, employment in the mining industry is strongly affected by changes in overall economic activity. In a recession the demand for coal drops, and many miners may be laid off.

For More Information

For free student materials about coal, electricity, and land reclamation issues, contact:

American Coal Foundation
1130 17th Street, NW, Suite 220
Washington, DC 20036-4604
Tel: 202-466-8630
Email: acf-coal@mindspring.com
Web: http://www.acf-coal.org/

For additional career information, contact the following organizations:

National Mining Association
1130 17th Street, NW
Washington, DC 20036
Email: rmaddalena@nma.org
Web: http://www.nma.org/

Society for Mining, Metallurgy, and Exploration
8307 Shaffer Parkway
Littleton, CO 80127
Tel: 800-763-3132
Web: http://www.smenet.org

The following labor union represents coal miners. For information on publications, press releases, and other resources, contact:

United Mine Workers of America
8315 Lee Highway
Fairfax, VA 22031
Tel: 703-208-7200
Web: http://www.umwa.org/

Energy Conservation Technicians

Overview

Energy conservation technicians identify and measure the amount of energy used to heat, cool, and operate a building or industrial process. They analyze the efficiency of energy use to determine the amount of energy lost through wasteful processes or lack of insulation. After analysis, they suggest energy conservation techniques and install any needed corrective measures.

History

At the start of the 20th century, energy costs were only a fraction of the total expense of operating homes, offices, and factories. Coal and petroleum were abundant and relatively inexpensive. Low energy prices contributed to the emergence of the United States as the leading industrialized nation as well as the world's largest energy consumer.

Because petroleum was inexpensive and could easily produce heat, steam, electricity, and fuel, it displaced coal for many purposes. As a result, the nation's coal mining industry declined, and the United States became dependent on foreign oil for half of its energy supply.

In 1973, when many foreign oil producing nations stopped shipments of oil to the United States and other Western countries, fuel costs increased dramatically. Although increased domestic oil production and decreased reliance on imports have since resulted in more stable prices, uncertainty about imported energy supplies remains. This uncertainty and a growing awareness about environmental pollution have fueled the development of energy conservation techniques in the United States. The emphasis on discovering new sources of energy, developing more efficient methods and equipment to use energy, and reducing the amount of wasted energy has created a demand for energy conservation technicians.

The Job

Energy efficiency and conservation are major concerns in nearly all homes and workplaces. This means that work assignments for energy conservation technicians vary greatly. They may inspect homes, businesses, or industrial buildings to identify conditions that cause energy waste, recommend ways to reduce the waste, and help install corrective measures. When technicians complete an analysis of a problem in energy use and effectiveness, they can state the results in tangible dollar costs, losses, or savings. Their work provides a basis for important decisions on using and conserving energy.

Energy conservation technicians may be employed in power plants, research laboratories, construction firms, industrial facilities, government agencies, or companies that sell and service equipment. The jobs these technicians perform can be divided into four major areas of energy activity: research and development, production, use, and conservation.

In research and development, technicians usually work in laboratories testing mechanical, electrical, chemical, pneumatic, hydraulic, thermal, or optical scientific principles. Typical employers include institutions, private industry, government, and the military. Working under the direction of an engineer, physicist, chemist, or metallurgist, technicians use specialized equipment and materials to perform laboratory experiments. They help record data and analyze it using computers. They may also be responsible for periodic maintenance and repair of equipment.

In energy production, typical employers include solar energy equipment manufacturers, installers, and users; power plants; and process plants that use high-temperature heat, steam, or water. Technicians in this field work with engineers and managers to develop, install, operate, maintain, and repair systems and devices used for the conversion of fuels or other resources into useful energy. Such plants may produce hot water, steam, mechanical motion, or electrical power through systems such as furnaces, electrical power plants, and solar heating systems. These systems may be controlled manually by semiautomated control panels or by computers.

In the field of energy use, technicians might work to improve efficiency in industrial engineering and production line equipment. They also maintain equipment and buildings for hospitals, schools, and multifamily housing.

Technicians working in energy conservation typically work for manufacturing companies, consulting engineers, energy-audit firms, and energy-audit departments of public utility companies. They are also hired by municipal governments, hotels, architects, private builders, and manufacturers of heating, ventilating, and air-conditioning equipment. Working in teams under engineers, technicians determine building specifications, modify equipment and structures, audit energy use and the efficiency of machines and systems, then recommend modifications or changes to save energy.

If working for a utility company, a technician might work as part of a demandside management (DSM) program, which helps customers reduce the amount of their electric bill. Under DSM programs, energy conservation technicians visit customers' homes to interview them about household energy use, such as the type of heating system, the number of people home during the day, the furnace temperature setting, and prior heating costs.

Technicians then draw a sketch of the house, measure its perimeter, windows, and doors, and record dimensions on the sketch. They inspect attics, crawl spaces, and basements and note any loose-fitting windows, uninsulated pipes, and deficient insulation. They read hot-water tank labels to find the heat-loss rating and determine the need for a tank insulation blanket. Technicians also examine air furnace filters and heat exchangers to detect dirt or soot buildup that might affect furnace operations. Once technicians identify a problem, they must know how to correct it. After discussing problems with the customer, the technician recommends repairs and provides literature on conservation improvements and sources of loans.

Requirements

High School

If you are interested in this field, take classes such as algebra, geometry, physics, chemistry, machine shop, and ecology. These courses and others incorporating laboratory work will provide you with a solid foundation for any postsecondary program that follows. In addition, classes in computer science, drafting (either mechanical or architectural), and public speaking are also very helpful.

Postsecondary Training

Many community colleges and technical institutes provide two-year programs under the specific title of energy conservation and use technology or energy management technology. In addition, schools offer related programs in solar power, electric power, building maintenance, equipment maintenance, and general engineering technology. Though not required for many entry-level jobs, these postsecondary programs can expand career options. With an advanced degree, applicants have a better chance at higher paying jobs, often with private industries.

Advanced training focuses on the principles and applications of physics, energy conservation, energy economics, instrumentation, electronics, electromechanical systems, computers, heating systems, and air-conditioning. A typical curriculum offers a first year of study in physics, chemistry, mathematics, energy technology, energy production systems, electricity and electromechanical devices, and microcomputer operations. The second year of study becomes more specialized, including courses in mechanical and fluid systems, electrical power, blueprint reading, energy conservation, codes and regulations, technical communications, and energy audits.

Considerable time is spent in laboratories, where students gain hands-on experience by assembling, disassembling, adjusting, and operating devices, mechanisms, and integrated systems of machines and controls.

Certification or Licensing

There are no state or federal requirements for certification or licensing of energy conservation technicians. However, a certificate from the National Institute for Certification in Engineering Technologies and a degree from an accredited technical program are valuable credentials and proof of knowledge and technical skills.

Other Requirements

Students entering this field must have a practical understanding of the physical sciences, a good aptitude for math, and the ability to communicate in writing and speech with technical specialists as well as average consumers. Their work requires a clear and precise understanding of operational and maintenance manuals, schematic drawings, blueprints, and computational formulas.

Some positions in electrical power plants require energy conservation technicians to pass certain psychological tests to predict their behavior during crises. Security clearances, arranged by the employer, are required for employment in nuclear power plants and other workplaces designated by the government as high-security facilities.

Exploring

To learn more about this profession, ask your career guidance counselor for additional information or for assistance in arranging a field trip to an industrial, commercial, or business workplace to further explore energy efficiency.

Utility companies exist in almost every city and employ energy analysts or a team of auditors in their customer service departments. Energy specialists also work for large hospitals, office buildings, hotels, universities, and manufacturing plants. Contact these employers of energy technicians to learn about opportunities for volunteer, part-time, or summer work.

You can also enroll in seminars offered by community colleges or equipment and material suppliers to learn about such topics as building insulation and energy sources. Student projects in energy conservation or part-time work with social service agencies that help low-income citizens meet their energy costs are other options for exploration.

Employers

Energy conservation technicians are employed in areas where much energy is used, such as power plants, research laboratories, construction firms, industrial facilities, government agencies, and companies that sell and service equipment. Technicians that focus on research and development work for institutions, private industry, government, and the military. Those that work in energy use are employed by manufacturing facilities, consulting engineering firms, energy audit firms, and energy audit departments of utility companies. Other employers include municipal governments, manufacturers of heating and cooling equipment, private builders, hotels, and architects.

Starting Out

Most graduates of technical programs are able to secure jobs in energy conservation before graduation by working with their schools' placement offices. Placement staffs work closely with potential employers, especially those that have hired graduates in recent years. Many large companies schedule regular recruiting visits to schools before graduation.

It is also possible to enter the field of energy conservation on the basis of work experience. People with a background in construction, plumbing, insulation, or heating may enter this field with the help of additional training to supplement their past work experience. Training in military instrumentation and systems control and maintenance is also good preparation for the prospective energy conservation technician. Former navy technicians are particularly sought in the field of energy production.

Opportunities for on-the-job training in energy conservation are available through part-time or summer work in hospitals, major office buildings, hotel chains, and universities. Some regions have youth corps aimed at high school students, such as the Youth Energy Corps (YEC) in New York City's South Bronx. The YEC offers high school dropouts the option of combining work experience and school to earn a general equivalency diploma, get a job, or both.

Some jobs in energy production, such as those in electrical power plants, can be obtained right out of high school. New employees, however, are expected to successfully complete company-sponsored training courses to keep up to date and advance to positions with more responsibility. Graduates with associate's degrees in energy conservation and use, instrumentation, electronics, or electromechanical technology will normally enter employment at a higher level, with more responsibility and higher pay, than those with less education. Jobs in energy research and development almost always require an associate's degree.

Advancement

Because the career is relatively new, well-established patterns of advancement have not yet emerged. Nevertheless, technicians in any of the four areas of energy conservation can advance to higher positions, such as senior and supervisory positions. These advanced positions require a combination of formal education, work experience, and special seminars or classes usually sponsored or paid for by the employer.

Technicians can also advance by progressing to new, more challenging assignments. For example, hotels, restaurants, and retail stores hire experienced energy technicians to manage energy consumption. This often involves visits to each location to audit and examine its facilities or procedures to see where energy use can be reduced. The technician then provides training in energy-saving practices. Other experienced energy technicians may be employed as sales and customer service representatives for producers of power, energy, special control systems, or equipment designed to improve energy efficiency.

Technicians with experience and money to invest may start their own businesses, selling energy-saving products, providing audits, or recommending energy-efficient renovations.

Earnings

Earnings of energy conservation technicians vary significantly based on the amount of formal training and experience. According to the U.S. Department of Labor, the median annual salary for engineering technicians was $37,310 in 1998. The lowest paid 10 percent earned less than $22,230 and the highest paid 10 percent earned more than $68,720. Average starting salaries with the federal government were lower than those in the private sector, ranging from $18,600 to $21,200 to $25,000 in 1999.

Technicians typically receive paid vacations, group insurance benefits, and employee retirement plans. In addition, their employers often offer financial support for all or part of continuing educational programs, which are necessary in order for technicians to keep up to date with technological changes that occur in this developing field.

Work Environment

Because energy conservation technicians are employed in many different settings, the environment in which they work varies widely. Energy conservation technicians employed in research and development, design, or product planning generally work in laboratories or engineering departments with normal daytime work schedules. Other technicians often travel to customer locations or work in their employer's plant.

Work in energy production and use requires around-the-clock shifts. In these two areas, technicians work either indoors or outdoors at the employer's site. Such assignments require little or no travel, but the work environments may be dirty, noisy, or affected by the weather. Appropriate work clothing must be worn in shop and factory settings, and safety awareness and safe working habits must be practiced at all times.

Energy conservation technicians who work in a plant usually interact with only a small group of people, but those who work for utility companies may have to communicate with the public while providing technical services to their customers. Energy research and development jobs involve laboratory activities requiring social interaction with engineers, scientists, and other technicians. In some cases, technicians may be considered public relations representatives, which may call for special attention to dress and overall appearance.

Job stress varies depending on the job. The pace is relaxed but businesslike in engineering, planning, and design departments and in research and development. However, in more hectic areas, technicians must respond to crisis situations involving unexpected breakdowns of equipment that must be corrected as soon as possible.

Outlook

Since energy use constitutes a major expense for industry, commerce, government, institutions, and private citizens, the demand for energy conservation technicians is likely to remain strong. The U.S. Department of Labor predicts that the employment of engineering technicians is expected to increase about as fast as the average for all occupations through 2008. In addition to the financial costs of purchasing natural resources, the added reality of the physical costs of depleting these important resources continues to create a greater demand for trained energy conservation employees. However, employment is influenced by local and national economic conditions.

The utilities industry is in the midst of significant regulatory and institutional changes. Government regulations are moving utility companies towards deregulation, opening new avenues for energy service companies. In the past, energy conservation programs have been dominated by people with engineering and other technical skills. These skills will remain important, but as the industry becomes more customer focused, there will be a growing need for more people with marketing and financial skills.

Utility companies, manufacturers, and government agencies are working together to establish energy efficiency standards. The Consortium for Energy Efficiency is a collaborative effort involving a group of electric and gas utility companies, government energy agencies, and environmental groups working to develop programs aimed at improving energy efficiency in commercial air-conditioning equipment, lighting, geothermal heat pumps, and other systems. Programs such as these will create job opportunities for technicians.

Utility demandside management (DSM) programs, which have traditionally concentrated on the residential sector, are now focusing more attention on industrial and commercial facilities. With the goal of realizing larger energy savings, lower costs, and more permanent energy-efficient changes, DSM programs are expanding to work with contractors, builders, retailers, distributors, and manufacturers, creating more demand for technicians.

For More Information

This trade association represents employees in the entire petroleum industry. For free videos, fact sheets, and informational booklets available to educators, contact:

American Petroleum Institute
1220 L Street, NW
Washington, DC 20005-4070
Tel: 202-682-8000
Web: http://www.api.org

For information on technical seminars, certification programs, conferences, books, and journals, contact:

Association of Energy Engineers
4025 Pleasantdale Road, Suite 420
Atlanta, GA 30340
Tel: 770-447-5083
Web: http://www.aeecenter.org

For information on certification programs for engineering technicians and technologists, contact:

National Institute for Certification in Engineering Technologies
1420 King Street
Alexandria, VA 22314-2794
Tel: 888-476-4238
Web: http://www.nicet.org

Energy Transmission and Distribution Workers

Overview

Energy transmission and distribution workers are employed in the electric light and power industry. They operate and maintain power-regulating equipment and networks of high-voltage power lines that send electricity from power plants to domestic, industrial, and commercial users.

History

Electricity was developed as a source of power during the 19th century, when a variety of technological advances made large-scale production of electricity feasible. The development of the first electric light bulb played an important role in the early growth of the electric power industry. Thomas Edison (1847-1931) demonstrated his first carbon filament lamp in 1879, and by

1882, the first permanent, commercial electric power-generating plant and distribution network was established in New York City. Other generating plants and power line networks soon followed in Europe and America. These early systems proved to be inefficient at transmitting power over long distances because they used direct electric current, but generators that produced alternating current became practical in the 1890s. Many new uses for electric power were developed, and by the early 1900s, electric-powered devices were increasingly common in homes, businesses, and factories across the United States.

Other advances, such as the development of oil-insulated transformers, also contributed to delivering electric power over great distances. In 1914, it was possible to send 150,000 volts over aerial transmission lines. There were problems, however, in the underground transmission of power. Several procedures were tried and dismissed, but the development of lead-sheathed cable in 1925 made it possible to transmit more than 100,000 volts underground.

Today, electric power generated at central power stations is sent to substations, then on to consumers via overhead lines, underground and submarine cables, and microwave systems. At generating stations or nearby substations, voltages must be stepped up so that less power is lost through resistance as the electricity is transmitted over long distances. Transformers in substations at the end of long transmission lines must decrease voltage to levels that are suitable for distribution to users.

The Job

Various workers are involved in regulating and directing electric power as it flows from the generators to consumers. The basic concern these workers share is maintaining a continuous and uninterrupted flow of energy, regardless of changing conditions and any problems that arise in the transmission and distribution system.

Substation operators monitor and regulate the flow of electricity at various facilities. At some substations located close to power plants, voltage may be stepped up for long distance transmission. Operators at these substations observe and record readings of instruments and meters that provide data on the electricity as it comes into and flows out of the substation.

At other substations at the end of long lines, where the voltage is stepped down again, the operators ensure that the equipment reduces the voltage for use by local consumers. Substation operators keep in touch with the main generating plant and connect or break the flow of electricity using levers that control circuit breakers. In substations where alternating current is changed to direct current to meet needs of special users, operators control converters that make these changes.

Some operators monitor equipment at several substations. Increasingly, the activities of substation operators are being automated so that the flow of electricity at various substations can be monitored and regulated from a central location.

Power dispatchers and distributors, also called *load dispatchers* or *systems operators,* control the transmission of power that is sent out from power plants. They work in rooms that function like command posts for coordinating the generating and distributing activities. These dispatchers monitor readings at a pilot board, which is like an automated map that displays everything that is happening throughout the entire transmission system. Instruments, meters, and lights on the pilot board show the status of transmission circuits, connections with substations, and the power draw by large industrial users. Based on this information, load dispatchers operate current converters, voltage transformers, and circuit breakers.

They also anticipate power needs, based on previous patterns of power use and variable factors such as weather conditions, and inform operators in the central control room of the generating plant about how much power will be needed at a later time. For example, if a hot day is forecast, load dispatchers know that consumers will be putting air-conditioners, fans, and refrigerators to maximum use and that enough power will have to be generated to meet the demand. In other instances, they may tell control room operators to produce less electricity when demand levels drop. In the event of emergencies such as equipment failures, they redirect the power flow around the problem until the situation is corrected. They may also operate equipment to adjust voltage up or down at substations and to control power flow in and out of the substations.

Utility lineworkers, also known as *line installers,* install, maintain, and repair poles, power lines, and other equipment that is part of the system for transmitting and distributing electricity from power plants to substations and to consumers. They may work alone or with small crews. To install poles in the ground, they may use power equipment to dig holes and set in the poles. They ride buckets on trucks with pneumatic lifts or sometimes climb the telephone poles to attach wires and cables to poles. Other responsibilities may include bolting or clamping insulators, lightning arresters, transformers, circuit breakers, switches, or other equipment.

With the help of other workers, installers string wires between poles or to buildings, adjusting the slack so that the lines do not break in changing weather conditions. They splice cables and attach wires to auxiliary equipment, using various hand tools. For underground cable installations, they may need to dig holes using special power equipment, such as trenchers and plows. Electric companies often contract out the job of installing high transmission towers to companies that specialize in such jobs, but utility lineworkers also may be involved in this work.

Ground helpers aid in setting up electric lines. Working as members of installation and repair crews, they dig holes, raise poles, and string lines. They may also pass the correct tools and equipment to installers and compact earth around the base of newly erected poles to hold them firmly in place.

Troubleshooters are experienced lineworkers who respond to emergency situations that require quick diagnosis and repair. They must be familiar with the power system and the various kinds of malfunctions that may develop. When they receive a call from a dispatcher, troubleshooters go to the area where the malfunction is reported. They examine the equipment and use testing devices to locate and assess the problem. They repair or replace conductors, switches, fuses, transformers, and related equipment. When they work with electrically energized lines, they use special safety methods and insulated ladders, tools, and platforms.

Cable splicers install and repair cables, especially in urban areas where cables are installed underground because above-ground power lines are impractical. Cable splicers pull cable through conduits, or ducts, that contain wires and join the cables at connecting points, according to diagrams and specifications. Also, they insulate the splice and seal it with a protective covering. They use testing devices to detect broken cables and incorrect connections, and they reinsulate or replace defective connections and cables.

Requirements

High School

For entry-level positions such as lineworkers, employers generally prefer high school graduates who can demonstrate mechanical aptitude and good mathematical, verbal, and reasoning skills on tests they administer. Applicants may also need to pass physical tests of balance, coordination, and strength. In high school, take courses in electrical shop, machine shop, drafting, and applied sciences.

Postsecondary Training

Utility lineworkers and cable splicers usually learn their skills in apprenticeship programs, which are administered jointly by employers and unions that organize company workers. Apprenticeships, which last several years, combine on-the-job training with formal instruction in related subjects. Apprentices attend classes to learn such subjects as blueprint reading, electrical theory, transmission theory, electrical codes, and job safety practices. In many programs, apprentices supplement class work with educational videos and computer-assisted instructional materials. They also get practical experience as helpers to experienced lineworkers. They begin by doing simple tasks and, as they learn, take on progressively more difficult work.

Load dispatchers and substation operators need a background that includes good training in sciences and mathematics, as well as years of job experience with the company. College-level courses are desirable.

Other Requirements

You should be comfortable working at heights. You also need to have good color vision to be able to distinguish color-coded wires and have a basic understanding of the principles of electricity.

Exploring

You can pursue your interest in subjects related to these occupations by taking courses such as physics and drafting. Shop courses can provide you with an opportunity to work with electrical and mechanical devices and to develop skills in schematic drawing. Some power plants have visitors' centers where the public is allowed to observe some of the plant operations and to learn how electricity is generated and distributed to consumers.

Employers

Energy transmission and distribution workers are typically employed by electric light and power companies. They may find jobs anywhere there is a power plant. Other workers are employed by manufacturing plants that produce their own electricity for use inhouse.

Starting Out

Load dispatchers and substation operators usually start off in other positions, perhaps entering as helpers or assistants. Depending on the openings that develop, the workers' preferences, and results of aptitude tests, they may be assigned to training for work as a substation operator. Load dispatchers may be chosen from among experienced substation operators. The training for load dispatchers is extensive, lasting several years. After completing initial training, dispatchers usually participate in periodic refresher training to update their skills.

Advancement

Advancement in these occupations is often related to length of experience and to receiving additional training at the company. Thus, with experience and training, ground helpers, for example, can become utility lineworkers. Experienced lineworkers, including utility lineworkers and cable splicers, may be promoted to supervisory positions. Expert utility lineworkers may become troubleshooters.

Load dispatchers and substation operators are promoted to these positions from other jobs inside the plant. Most of these workers continue to advance within the same plant or utility and eventually may become shift supervisors.

Earnings

Earnings of workers in these occupations vary considerably depending on specific job responsibilities, length of service with the company, geographic region, and other factors. On average, workers in the electric utility industry have relatively competitive earnings.

Power generating plant operators earned a median salary of $44,840 in 1998, according to the U.S. Department of Labor. The highest paid 10 percent earned more than $73,090 a year, while the lowest paid 10 percent of workers earned less than $29,000. The majority of power distributors and dispatchers earned between $37,350 and $56,810 annually in 1998. Most utility lineworkers earn between $34,000 and $50,000 a year, although starting salaries are usually somewhat lower. Utility lineworkers and other workers who are union members generally have their pay rates set according to agreements between the union and their employer. The agreements cover many factors, such as wage increases and pay rates for different categories of overtime work. Overtime pay can add significantly to base salary. In addition to their regular earnings, these workers receive benefits such as paid vacation time, pension plans, and life and health insurance.

Work Environment

Workers who install and repair electric power lines encounter a variety of conditions on the job. They often work outdoors in all kinds of weather. They may have to climb to high places or work in awkward positions, such as stooped over in damp underground tunnels. They may have to lift heavy cables. As they work, they must always be aware of safety issues and follow procedures that minimize the risk of injury. Lines energized with electricity can cause burns or fatal electric shocks. Workers who go into underground tunnels have to use special safety equipment and test for the presence of gas in the air. Some workers risk being exposed to hazardous chemicals in solvents and other materials. Other potential risks include being hit by objects falling from overhead at a worksite.

Even during their off hours, installation and repair workers may have to be available for emergency repairs. After a major storm, for example, they may have to work long hours and travel great distances to help repair equipment and restore service to customers.

In facilities where power flow is monitored and regulated, workers enjoy clean, orderly, well-lighted, and ventilated control rooms. Their work is not strenuous, but they must constantly pay attention to the equipment that indicates how the system is functioning. Since electricity must be provided to consumers all the time, they must work some shifts at night, on weekends, and on holidays, often on a rotating basis.

Outlook

The U.S. Department of Labor reports that employment for transmission and distribution workers will decline slightly through 2008, in part because of industry deregulation and increased competition between electric light and power companies. In addition, technological improvements have made some equipment more efficient and reliable, and the use of automatic controls is reducing the need for people to monitor and regulate transmission and distribution systems. Much work that power utility lineworkers do is not as readily automated, and many openings for these workers will continue to develop as experienced workers transfer to other jobs or leave the workforce.

For More Information

For information on energy issues and a list of available publications, contact:

Edison Electric Institute
701 Pennsylvania Avenue, NW
Washington, DC 20004-2696
Tel: 202-508-5000
Web: http://www.eei.org

For information on union representation, contact:

International Brotherhood of Electrical Workers
1125 15th Street, NW
Washington, DC 20005
Tel: 202-833-7000
Web: http://www.ibew.org/

For a fun overview of the energy industry, visit the following Web site:

U.S. Energy Information Administration's Kid's Page
Web: http://www.eia.doe.gov/kids/

Geologists

Overview

Geologists study all aspects of the earth, including its origin, history, composition, and structure. Along more practical lines, geologists may, through the use of theoretical knowledge and research data, locate groundwater, oil, minerals, and other natural resources. They play an increasingly important role in studying, preserving, and cleaning up the environment. They advise construction companies and government agencies on the suitability of locations being considered for buildings, highways, and other structures. They also prepare geological reports, maps, and diagrams. There are approximately 44,000 geologists, geophysicists, and oceanographers employed in the United States, according to the U.S. Department of Labor.

History

Geology is a young science, first developed by early mining engineers. In the late 18th century, scientists such as A. G. Werner and James Hutton, a retired British physician, created a sensation with their differing theories on the origins of rocks. Through the study of fossils and the development of geological maps, others continued to examine the history of the earth in the 19th century.

From these beginnings, geology has made rapid advances, both in scope and knowledge. With the development of more intricate technology, geologists are able to study areas of the earth they were previously unable to reach. Seismographs, for example, measure energy waves resulting from the earth's movement in order to determine the location and intensity of earthquakes. Seismic prospecting involves bouncing sound waves off buried rock layers.

The Job

The geologist's work includes locating and obtaining physical data and material. This may necessitate the drilling of deep holes to obtain samples, the collection and examination of the materials found on or under the earth's surface, or the use of instruments to measure the earth's gravity and magnetic field. Some geologists may spend three to six months of each year in fieldwork. In laboratory work, geologists carry out studies based on field research. Sometimes working under controlled temperatures or pressures, geologists analyze the chemical and physical properties of geological specimens, such as rock, fossil remains, and soil. Once the data is analyzed and the studies are completed, geologists, and geological technicians write reports based on their research.

A wide variety of laboratory instruments are used, including X-ray diffractometers, which determine the crystal structure of minerals, and petrographic microscopes for the study of rock and sediment samples.

Geologists working to protect the environment may design and monitor waste disposal sites, preserve water supplies, and reclaim contaminated land and water to comply with more stringent federal environmental regulations.

Geologists often specialize in one of the following disciplines:

Marine geologists study the oceans, including the seabed and subsurface features.

Paleontologists specialize in the study of the earth's rock formations, including remains of plant and animal life, in order to understand the earth's evolution and estimate its age.

Geochronologists use radioactive dating and other techniques to estinate the age of rocks and other samples from an exploration site.

Petroleum geologists attempt to locate natural gas and oil deposits through exploratory testing and study of the data obtained. They recommend the acquisition of new properties and the retention or release of properties already owned by their companies. They also estimate oil reserves and assist petroleum engineers in determining exact production procedures.

Closely related to petroleum geologists are *economic geologists,* who search for new resources of minerals and fuels.

Engineering geologists are responsible for the application of geological knowledge to problems arising in the construction of roads, buildings, bridges, dams, and other structures.

Mineralogists are interested in the classification of minerals composing rocks and mineral deposits. To this end, they examine and analyze the physical and chemical properties of minerals and precious stones to develop data and theories on their origin, occurrence, and possible uses in industry and commerce.

Petrologists study the origin of igneous, metamorphic, and sedimentary rocks.

Stratigraphers study the distribution and relative arrangement of sedimentary rock layers. This enables them to understand evolutionary changes in fossils and plants, which leads to an understanding of successive changes in the distribution of land and sea.

Closely related to stratigraphers are *sedimentologists,* who determine processes and products involved in sedimentary rock formations.

Geohydrologists study the nature and distribution of water within the earth and are often involved in environmental impact studies.

Geomorphologists study the form of the earth's surface and the processes, such as erosion and glaciation, that bring about changes.

Glacial geologists study the physical properties and movement of ice sheets and glaciers.

The geologist is far from limited in a choice of work, but a basic knowledge of all sciences is essential in each of these specializations. An increasing number of scientists combine geology with detailed knowledge in another field. *Geochemists,* for example, are concerned with the chemical composition of, and the changes in, minerals and rocks, while *planetary geologists* apply their knowledge of geology to interpret surface conditions on the Moon and other planets.

Requirements

High School

In high school, you should study earth science, physics, computer science, geography, social studies, mathematics, and English.

Postsecondary Training

A bachelor's degree is the minimum requirement for entry into lower-level geology jobs, but a master's degree is usually necessary for beginning positions in research, teaching, and exploration. A person with a strong background in physics, chemistry, mathematics, or computer science may also qualify for some geology jobs. For those wishing to make significant advancements in research and for teaching at the college level, a doctoral degree is required. Those interested in the geological profession should have an aptitude not only for geology but also for physics, chemistry, and mathematics.

A number of colleges, universities, and institutions of technology offer degrees in geology. Programs in geophysical technology, geophysical engineering, geophysical prospecting, and engineering geology also offer related training for beginning geologists.

Traditional geoscience courses emphasize classical geologic methods and concepts. Mineralogy, paleontology, stratigraphy, and structural geology are important courses for undergraduates. Students interested in environmental and regulatory fields should take courses in hydrology, hazardous waste management, environmental legislation, chemistry, fluid mechanics, and geologic logging.

In addition, students should take courses in related sciences, mathematics, English composition, and computer science. Students seeking graduate degrees in geology concentrate on advanced courses in geology, placing major emphasis on their particular fields.

Certification or Licensing

Twenty-six states require geologists to be licensed. Most of these states require applicants (who have earned a bachelor's degree in the geological sciences) to pass the Fundamentals of Geology exam, a standardized written exam developed by the Association of State Boards of Geology.

The American Institute of Professional Geologists grants the Certified Professional Geologist (CPG) designation to geologists who have earned a bachelor's degree or higher in the geological sciences and have eight years of professional experience (applicants with a master's degree need only seven years of professional experience and those with a Ph.D., five years). Candidates must also undergo peer review by three professional geologists (two of whom must be CPGs) and pay an application fee.

The Institute also offers the Registered Member designation to geologists who are registered in various states and are not seeking certification. Applicants must have at least a bachelor's degree, be licensed by the state they wish to work in, undergo peer review, and pay an application fee.

Other Requirements

In addition to academic training and work experience, geologists who work in the field or in administration must have skills in business administration and in working with other people. Computer modeling, data processing, and effective oral and written communication skills are important, as well as the ability to think independently and creatively. Physical stamina is needed for those involved in fieldwork.

Exploring

If this career sounds interesting, try to read as much as possible about geology and geologists. Your best chance for association with geologists and geological work is to join the clubs or organizations concerned with such things as rock collecting. Amateur geological groups and local museums also offer opportunities for you to gain exposure to the field of geology.

Employers

The majority of geologists are employed in private industry. Some work for oil and gas extraction and mining companies, primarily in exploration. The rest work for business service, environmental and geotechnical consulting firms, or they are self-employed as consultants to industry and government. The federal government employs geologists in the Department of the Interior (in the U.S. Geological Survey, the Bureau of Mines, or the Bureau of Reclamation) and in the Departments of Defense, Agriculture, and Commerce. Geologists also work for state agencies, nonprofit research organizations, and museums. Many geologists hold faculty positions at colleges and universities and most of these combine their teaching with research.

Starting Out

After completing sufficient educational requirements, preferably a master's degree or doctorate, the geologist may look for work in various areas, including private industry and government. For those who wish to teach at the college level, a doctorate is required. College graduates may also take government civil service examinations or possibly find work on state geological surveys, which are sometimes based on civil service competition.

Geologists often begin their careers in field exploration or as research assistants in laboratories. As they gain experience, they are given more difficult assignments and may be promoted to supervisory positions, such as project leader or program manager.

Advancement

The geologist with a bachelor's degree has little chance of advancing to higher-level positions. Continued formal training and work experience are necessary, especially as competition for these positions grows more intense. A doctorate is essential for most college or university teaching positions and is preferred for much research work.

Earnings

Beginning geologists with a bachelor's degree earned about $34,900 annually in 1999, according to the National Association of Colleges and Employers. Those with a master's degrees received an average starting salary of $44,700. The U.S. Department of Labor reports that the median annual salary for geologists, oceanographers, and geophysicists was $53,890 in 1998; the top paid

10 percent earned more than $101,390, while the lowest paid 10 percent earned less than $30,950 a year.

In the federal government, the average salary for geologists in managerial, supervisory, and nonsupervisory positions was $64,400 a year in 1999; for geophysicists, $72,500; for hydrologists, $58,900; and for oceanographers, $66,000.

Although the petroleum, mineral, and mining industries offer higher salaries, competition for these jobs is stiff, and there is less job security than in other areas. In addition, college and university teachers can earn additional income through research, writing, and consulting. Salaries for foreign assignments may range significantly higher than those in the United States.

Work Environment

Some geologists spend most of their time in a laboratory or office, working a regular 40-hour week in pleasant conditions; others divide their time between fieldwork and office or laboratory work. Those who work in the field often travel to remote sites by helicopter or four-wheel drive vehicle and cover large areas on foot. They may camp for extended periods of time in primitive conditions with the members of the geological team as their only companions. Some geologists work overseas or in remote areas, and job relocation is not unusual. Others, such as marine geologists may spend considerable time at sea.

Outlook

According to the *Occupational Outlook Handbook*, employment of geologists is expected to grow about as fast as the average for all occupations through 2008. In addition to the oil and gas industries, geologists will be able to find jobs in environmental protection and reclamation. Government agencies will have fewer jobs available because of cutbacks.

In response to the curtailed petroleum activity in the late 1980s and 1990s, the number of graduates in geology and geophysics, especially petroleum geology, dropped considerably in the last decade. Stability has now returned to the petroleum industry, increasing the need for qualified geoscientists. With new technologies and greater demand for energy resources, job opportunities are expected to be good, especially for those with a master's degree and those familiar with computer modeling and GPS (global positioning system). Geologists who are able to speak a foreign language and who are willing to work overseas will also have strong employment prospects.

For More Information

For information on geoscience careers, contact:

American Geological Institute
4220 King Street
Alexandria, VA 22302-1502
Tel: 703-379-2480
Web: http://www.agiweb.org

For information on certification, contact:

American Institute of Professional Geologists
8703 Yates Drive, Suite 200
Westminster, CO 80031-3681
Tel: 303-412-6205
Email: aipg@aipg.org
Web: http://www.aipg.org

For information on the Fundamentals of Geology exam, contact:

Association of State Boards of Geology
PO Box 11591
Columbia, SC 29211-1591
Tel: 803-799-1047
Email: asbog@asbog.org
Web: http://www.asbog.org/

For career information and job listings, contact:

Geological Society of America
PO Box 9140
Boulder, CO 80301-9140
Tel: 303-447-2020
Email: educate@geosociety.org
Web: http://www.geosociety.org/

Geophysicists

Earth science Physics	School Subjects
Helping/teaching Technical/scientific	Personal Skills
Indoors and outdoors One location with some travel	Work Environment
Bachelor's degree	Minimum Education Level
$30,950 to $53,890 to $101,390+	Salary Range
None available	Certification or Licensing
About as fast as the average	Outlook

Overview

Geophysicists are concerned with matter and energy and how they interact. They study the physical properties and structure of the earth, from its interior to its upper atmosphere, including land surfaces, subsurfaces, and bodies of water. There are approximately 44,000 geophysicists, geologists, and oceanographers employed in the United States, according to the U.S. Department of Labor.

History

Geophysics is an important field that combines the sciences of geology and physics. Geology is the study of the history and composition of the earth as recorded by rock formations and fossils. Physics deals with all forms of energy, the properties of matter, and the relationship between energy and matter. The geophysicist is an "earth physicist," one who works with the physical aspects of the earth from its inner core to outer space.

This alliance between the earth and physical sciences is part of the progress that science has made in searching for new understandings of the world. Like the fields of biochemistry, biomathematics, space medicine, and nuclear physics, geophysics combines the knowledge of two disciplines. However, the importance of geophysics goes well beyond abstract theory. Geophysicists apply their knowledge to such practical problems as predicting earthquakes, locating raw materials and sources of power, and evaluating sites for power plants.

The Job

Geophysicists use the principles and techniques of geology, physics, chemistry, mathematics, and engineering to perform tests and conduct research on the surface, atmosphere, waters, and solid bodies of the earth. They study seismic, gravitational, electrical, thermal, and magnetic phenomena to determine the structure and composition of the earth, as well as the forces causing movement and warping of the surface.

Many geophysicists are involved in fieldwork, where they engage in exploration and prospecting. Others work in laboratories, where research activities are the center of attention. In general, their instruments are highly complex and designed to take very precise measurements. Most geophysicists specialize in one of the following areas.

Geodesists measure the shape and size of the earth to determine fixed points, positions, and elevations on or near the earth's surface. Using the gravimeter, they perform surveys to measure minute variations in the earth's gravitational field. They also collect data that is useful in learning more about the weight, size, and mass of the earth. Geodesists are active in tracking satellites orbiting in outer space.

Geomagneticians use the magnetometer to measure variations in the earth's magnetic field from magnetic observatories and stations. They are also concerned with conditions affecting radio signals, solar phenomena, and many other aspects of space exploration. The data gathered can be most helpful in working with problems in radio and television transmission, telegraphy, navigation, mapping, and space exploration and space science.

Applied geophysicists use data gathered from the air and ground, as well as computers, to analyze the earth's crust. They look for oil and mineral deposits and try to find sites for the safe disposal of hazardous wastes.

Exploration geophysicists, sometimes called *geophysical prospectors,* use seismic techniques to look for possible oil and gas deposits. They may use sonar equipment to send sound waves deep into the earth. The resulting echo helps them estimate if an oil deposit lies hidden in the area.

Hydrologists are concerned with the surface and underground waters in the land areas of the earth. They map and chart the flow and the disposition of sediments, measure changes in water volume, and collect data on the form and intensity of precipitation, as well as on the disposition of water through evaporation and ground absorption. The information that the hydrologist collects is applied to problems in flood control, crop production, soil and water conservation, irrigation, and inland water projects. Some hydrologists study glaciers and their sedimentation.

Seismologists specialize in the study of earthquakes. With the aid of the seismograph and other instruments that record the location of earthquakes and the vibrations they cause, seismologists examine active fault lines and areas where earthquakes have occurred. They are often members of field teams whose purpose is to examine and evaluate possible building or construction sites. They also may explore for oil and minerals. In recent years, seismologists have contributed to the selection of missile launching sites.

Tectonophysicists study the structure of mountains and ocean basins, the properties of the earth's crust, and the physical forces and processes that cause movements and changes in the structure of the earth. A great deal of their work is research, and their findings are helpful in locating oil and mineral deposits.

Volcanologists study volcanoes, their location, and their activity. They are concerned with their origin and the phenomena of their processes.

Planetologists use data from artificial satellites and astronauts' equipment to study the makeup and atmosphere of the planets, the moon, and other bodies in our solar system. Recent advances in this field have greatly increased our knowledge of Jupiter, Saturn, and their satellites.

Requirements

High School

A strong interest in the physical and earth sciences is essential for this field. You should take basic courses in earth science, physics, chemistry, and at least four years of mathematics. Advanced placement work in any of the mathematics and sciences is also helpful. Other recommended courses include mechanical drawing, shop, social studies, English, and computer science.

Postsecondary Training

A bachelor's degree in geophysics is required for most entry-level positions. Physics, mathematics, and chemistry majors can locate positions in geophysics, but some work in geology is highly desirable and often required, especially for certain government positions.

Graduate work at the master's or doctoral level is required for research and college teaching positions and for positions of a policy-making or policy-interpreting nature in private or government employment.

Many colleges and universities offer a bachelor's degree in geophysics, and a growing number of these institutions also award advanced degrees. An undergraduate major in geophysics is not usually required for entrance into a graduate program.

Other Requirements

If you seek employment in the federal government you will have to take a civil service examination and be able to meet other specified requirements.

You should also possess a strong aptitude in mathematics and science, particularly the physical and earth sciences, and an interest in observing nature, performing experiments, and studying the physical environment. Because geophysicists frequently spend time outdoors, you should enjoy outdoor activities such as hiking and camping.

Exploring

You can explore various aspects of this field by taking earth and physical science courses. Units of study dealing with electricity, rocks and minerals, metals and metallurgy, the universe and space, and weather and climate may offer you an opportunity for further learning about the field. Hobbies that deal with radio, electronics, and rock or map collecting also offer opportunities to learn about the basic principles involved in geophysics.

Some colleges and universities have a student chapter of the Society of Exploration Geophysicists that you can join. Employment as an aide or helper with a geophysical field party may be available during the summer months and provide you with the opportunity to study the physical environment and interact with geophysicists.

Employers

Geophysicists are employed primarily by the petroleum industry, mining companies, exploration and consulting firms, and research institutions. A few geophysicists work as consultants, offering their services on a fee or contract basis. Many work for the federal government, mainly the Coast and Geodetic Survey, the U.S. Geological Survey, the Army Map Service, and the Naval Oceanographic Office. Other geophysicists pursue teaching careers.

Starting Out

Most college placement offices are prepared to help students locate positions in business, industry, or government agencies. Other job contacts can be made through professors, friends, and relatives. Some companies visit college campuses in the spring of each year to interview candidates who are interested in positions as geophysicists. The college placement office can usually provide helpful information on job opportunities in the field of geophysics.

Advancement

If employed by a private firm, a new employee with only a bachelor's degree will probably have an on-the-job training period. As a company trainee, the beginning geophysicist may be assigned to a number of different jobs. On a field party, the trainee will probably work with a junior geophysicist, which in many companies is the level of assignment received after the training has ended.

From a junior geophysicist, advancement is usually to intermediate geophysicist, and eventually to geophysicist. From this point, one can transfer to research positions or, if the geophysicist remains in fieldwork, to *party chief*. The party chief's job is to coordinate the work of people in a crew, including trainees, junior, intermediate, and full geophysicists, surveyors, observers, drillers, shooters, and aides. Advancement with the company may eventually lead to supervisory and management positions.

Geophysicists can often transfer to other jobs in the fields of geology, physics, and engineering, depending on their qualifications and experience.

Earnings

The salaries of geophysicists are comparable to the earnings of those in other scientific professions. According to the U.S. Department of Labor, geophysicists earned an average annual salary of $53,890 in 1998. The lowest paid 10 percent earned less than $30,950 per year, while the highest paid 10 percent earned over $101,390 annually. Additional compensation is awarded to those who are required to live outside the United States. In 1999, the average salary for a geophysicist working for the federal government was $72,500. The median annual salary for exploration geophysicists was $80,000 in 1998, according to a member survey conducted by the Society of Exploration Geophysicists.

Both the federal government and private industry provide additional benefits, including vacations, retirement pensions, health and life insurance, and sick leave benefits.

Positions in colleges and universities offer annual salaries ranging from about $28,000 for instructors to $65,000 for full professors. Salaries depend upon experience, education, and professional rank. Faculty members may teach in summer school for additional compensation and also engage in writing, consulting, and research for government, industry, or business.

Work Environment

Geophysicists employed in laboratories or offices generally work a regular 40-hour week under typical office conditions. Field geophysicists work under a variety of conditions and often the hours are irregular. They are outdoors much of the time in all kinds of weather. The work requires carrying small tools and equipment and occasionally some heavy lifting. The field geophysicist is often required to travel and work in isolated areas. Volcanologists, for example, may face dangerous conditions when visiting and gathering data near an erupting volcano.

Outlook

According to the *Occupational Outlook Handbook,* employment of geophysicists is expected to grow about as fast as the average through 2008. The total number of graduates with degrees in the geophysical sciences is expected to remain small and insufficient to meet the moderate increase in industry job openings. This may eventually result in fewer employment possibilities in college teaching.

The petroleum industry, the largest employer of geophysicists, has increased its exploration activities, and more geophysicists will be needed to locate less accessible fuel and mineral deposits and to do research on such problems as radioactivity, cosmic and solar radiation, and the use of geothermal energy to generate electricity. The petroleum industry is also expected to expand operations overseas, which may create new jobs for those who are willing to travel.

The federal government will need more geophysicists to study water, conservation, flood control, and other problems and to assist in space science projects. The growing need to find new sources of energy will undoubtedly make the work of geophysicists more important and more challenging in the next century.

For More Information

For information on geoscience careers, contact:

American Geological Institute
4220 King Street
Alexandria, VA 22302-1502
Tel: 703-379-2480
Web: http://www.agiweb.org

For information on local meetings, publications, job opportunities, and science news, contact:

American Geophysical Union
2000 Florida Avenue, NW
Washington, DC 20009-1277
Tel: 202-462-6900
Email: service@agu.org
Web: http://www.agu.org

For information on student chapters at colleges and universities and services for elementary and high school students, contact:

Society of Exploration Geophysicists
PO Box 702740
Tulsa, OK 74170-2740
Tel: 918-497-5500
Email: web@seg.org
Web: http://www.seg.org

Industrial Machinery Mechanics

School Subjects	Mathematics Technical/shop
Personal Skills	Mechanical/manipulative Technical/scientific
Work Environment	Primarily indoors Primarily one location
Minimum Education Level	Apprenticeship
Salary Range	$21,030 to $31,840 to $47,780
Certification or Licensing	None available
Outlook	Little change or more slowly than the average

Overview

Industrial machinery mechanics, often called *machinery maintenance mechanics* or *industrial machinery repairers,* inspect, maintain, repair, and adjust industrial production and processing machinery and equipment to ensure its proper operation in various industries. Approximately 535,000 industrial machinery mechanics work in the United States.

History

Before 1750 and the beginning of the Industrial Revolution in Europe, almost all work was done by hand. Families grew their own food, wove their own cloth, and bought or traded very little. Gradually the economic landscape changed. Factories mass-produced products that had once been created by hand. The spinning jenny, a multiple-spindle machine for spinning wool or cotton, was one of the first machines of the Industrial Revolution. After it came a long procession of inventions and developments, including the steam engine, power loom, cotton gin, steamboat, locomotive, telegraph, and Bessemer converter. With these machines came the need for people who could maintain and repair them.

Mechanics learned that all machines are based on six configurations: the lever, the wheel and axle, the pulley, the inclined plane, the wedge, and the screw. By combining these elements in more complex ways, the machines could do more work in less time than people or animals could do. Thus, the role of machinery mechanics became vital in keeping production lines running and businesses profitable.

The Industrial Revolution continues even today, although now it is known as the Age of Automation. As machines become more numerous and more complex, the work of the industrial machinery mechanic becomes even more necessary.

The Job

The types of machinery on which industrial machinery mechanics work are as varied as the types of industries operating in the United States today. Mechanics are employed in metal stamping plants, printing plants, chemical and plastics plants—almost any type of large-scale industrial operation that can be imagined. The machinery in these plants must be maintained regularly. Breakdowns and delays with one machine can hinder a plant's entire operation, which is costly for the company.

Preventive maintenance is a major part of mechanics' jobs. They inspect the equipment, oil and grease moving components, and clean and repair parts. They also keep detailed maintenance records on the equipment they service. They often follow blueprints and engineering specifications to maintain and fix equipment.

When breakdowns occur, mechanics may partially or completely disassemble a machine to make the necessary repairs. They replace worn bearings, adjust clutches, and replace and repair defective parts. They may have to order replacement parts from the machinery's manufacturer. If no parts are available, they may have to make the necessary replacements, using milling machines, lathes, or other tooling equipment. After the machine is reassembled, they may have to make adjustments to its operational settings. They often work with the machine's regular operator to test it. When repairing electronically controlled machinery, mechanics may work closely with electronic repairers or electricians who maintain the machine's electronic parts.

Often these mechanics can identify potential breakdowns and fix problems before any real damage or delays occur. They may notice that a machine is vibrating, rattling, or squeaking, or they may see that the items produced by the machine are flawed. Many types of new machinery are built with programmed internal evaluation systems that check the accuracy and condition of equipment. This assists mechanics in their jobs, but it also makes them responsible for maintaining the check-up systems.

Machinery installations are becoming another facet of a mechanic's job. As plants retool and invest in new equipment, they rely on mechanics to properly situate and install the machinery. In many plants, millwrights traditionally did this job, but as employers increasingly seek workers with multiple skills, industrial machinery mechanics are taking on new responsibilities.

Industrial machinery mechanics may use a wide range of tools when doing preventive maintenance or making repairs. For example, they may use simple tools such as a screwdriver and wrench to repair an engine or a hoist to lift a printing press off the ground. Sometimes they may have to solder or weld equipment. They use power and hand tools and precision measuring instruments. In some shops, mechanics troubleshoot for the entire plant's operations. Others may become experts in electronics, hydraulics, pneumatics, or other specialties.

Requirements

High School

While most employers prefer to hire those who have completed high school, opportunities do exist for those without a diploma as long as they have had some kind of related training. While you are in high school, take courses in mechanical drawing, general mathematics, algebra, and geometry. Other classes that will help prepare you for this career are physics, computers, and electronics. Any class that gives you experience in blueprint reading will add to your qualifications.

Postsecondary Training

In the past, most industrial machinery mechanics learned the skills of the trade informally by spending several years as helpers in a particular factory. Currently, as machinery has become more complex, more formal training is necessary. Today many mechanics learn the trade through apprenticeship programs sponsored by a local trade union. Apprenticeship programs usually last four years and include both on-the-job and related classroom training. In addition to the use and care of machine and hand tools, apprentices learn the operation, lubrication, and adjustment of the machinery and equipment they will maintain. In class they learn shop mathematics, blueprint reading, safety, hydraulics, welding, and other subjects related to the trade.

Students may also obtain training through vocational or technical schools. Useful programs are those that offer machine shop courses and provide training in electronics and numerical control machine tools.

Other Requirements

Students interested in this field should possess mechanical aptitude and manual dexterity. Good physical condition and agility are necessary because as a mechanic you will sometimes have to lift heavy objects, crawl under large machines, or climb to reach equipment located high above the factory floor.

Mechanics are responsible for valuable equipment and are often called upon to exercise considerable independent judgment. Because of technological advances, you should be willing to learn the requirements of new machines and production techniques. When a plant purchases new equipment, the equipment's manufacturer often trains plant employees in proper operation and maintenance. Technological change requires mechanics to have adaptability and inquiring minds.

Exploring

If you are interested in this field, you should take as many shop courses as you can. Exploring and repairing machinery, such as automobiles and home appliances, will also sharpen your skills. In addition, try landing part-time work or a summer job in an industrial plant that gives you the opportunity to observe industrial repair work being done.

Employers

Industrial machinery mechanics work in a wide variety of plants and are employed in every part of the country, although employment is concentrated in industrialized areas. According to the U.S. Department of Labor, most of the 535,000 industrial machinery mechanics work in industries such as food processing, textile mill products, chemicals, fabricated metal products, and primary metals. Others work for government agencies, public utilities, mining companies, and other facilities where industrial machinery is used.

Starting Out

Jobs can be obtained by directly applying to companies that use industrial equipment or machinery. The majority of mechanics work for manufacturing plants. These plants are found in a wide variety of industries, including the automotive, plastics, textile, electronics, packaging, food, beverage, and aerospace industries. Chances for job openings may be better at a large plant. New workers are generally assigned to work as helpers or trainees.

Prospective mechanics also may learn of job openings or apprenticeship programs through local unions. Industrial mechanics may be represented by one of several unions, depending on their industry and place of employment. These unions include the United Automobile, Aerospace and Agricultural Implement Workers of America; the United Steelworkers of America; the International Union of Electronic, Electrical, Salaried, Machine, and Furniture Workers; and the International Association of Machinists and Aerospace Workers. Private and state employment offices are other good sources of job openings.

Advancement

Those who begin as helpers or trainees usually become journeymen in four years. Although opportunities for advancement beyond this rank are somewhat limited, industrial machinery mechanics who learn more complicated machinery and equipment can advance into higher-paying positions. The most highly skilled mechanics may be promoted to master mechanics. Those who demonstrate good leadership and interpersonal skills can become supervisors. Skilled mechanics also have the option of becoming machinists, numerical control tool programmers, precision metalworkers, packaging machinery technicians, and robotics technicians. Some of these positions do require additional training, but the skills of a mechanic readily transfer to these areas.

Earnings

In 1998, the median annual earnings for industrial machinery mechanics was around $31,840, according to the U.S. Department of Labor. The lowest paid 10 percent of these mechanics earned about $21,030, while the highest paid 10 percent earned approximately $47,780 during that same period. Apprentices generally earn lower wages and earn incremental raises as they advance in their training. Earnings vary based on experience, skills, type of industry, and geographic location. For example, mechanics employed in the textile industry generally earn wages at the low end of the scale, with workers in the automotive, metalworking, and aircraft industries earning wages at the high end. Mechanics in the Midwest typically earn higher salaries than those in the South. Those working in union plants generally earn more than those in nonunion plants. Most industrial machinery mechanics are provided with benefit packages, which can include paid holidays and vacations; medical, dental, and life insurance; and retirement plans.

Work Environment

Industrial machinery mechanics work in all types of manufacturing plants, which may be hot, noisy, and dirty or relatively quiet and clean. Mechanics frequently work with greasy, dirty equipment and need to be able to adapt to a variety of physical conditions. Because machinery is not always accessible, mechanics may have to work in stooped or cramped positions or on high ladders.

Although working around machinery poses some danger, this risk is minimized with proper safety precautions. Modern machinery includes many safety features and devices, and most plants follow good safety practices. Mechanics often wear protective clothing and equipment, such as hard hats and safety belts, glasses, and shoes.

Mechanics work with little supervision and need to be able to work well with others. They need to be flexible and respond to changing priorities, which can result in interruptions that pull a mechanic off one job to repair a more urgent problem. Although the standard workweek is 40 hours, overtime is common. Because factories and other sites cannot afford breakdowns, industrial machinery mechanics may be called to the plant at night or on weekends for emergency repairs.

Outlook

The U.S. Department of Labor predicts that employment will grow more slowly than the average through 2008 for industrial machinery mechanics. Some industries will have a greater need for mechanics than others. Much of the new automated production equipment that companies are purchasing has its own self-diagnostic capabilities and is more reliable than older equipment. Although this machinery still needs to be maintained, most job openings will stem from the replacement of transferring or retiring workers.

Certain industries are extremely susceptible to changing economic factors and reduce production activities in slow periods. During these periods, companies may lay off workers or reduce hours. Mechanics are less likely to be laid off than other workers as machines need to be maintained regardless of production levels. Slower production periods and temporary shutdowns are often used to overhaul equipment. Nonetheless, employment opportunities are generally better at companies experiencing growth or stable levels of production.

Because machinery is becoming more complex and automated, mechanics need to be more highly skilled than in the past. Mechanics who stay up to date with new technologies, particularly those related to electronics and computers, will be best prepared to meet the needs of companies that use these workers.

For More Information

For information about scholarships, contact:

Association for Manufacturing Technology
7901 Westpark Drive
McLean, VA 22102
Tel: 703-893-2900
Web: http://www.mfgtech.org

For information about apprentice programs, contact UAW:

International Union, United Automobile, Aerospace and Agricultural Implement Workers of America (UAW)
8000 East Jefferson Avenue
Detroit, MI 48214
Tel: 313-926-5000
Web: http://www.uaw.org

For information about the machining industry and career opportunities, contact:

National Tooling and Machining Association
9300 Livingston Road
Fort Washington, MD 20744
Tel: 301-248-6200
Web: http://www.ntma.org

Line Installers and Cable Splicers

School Subjects
Mathematics
Technical/shop

Personal Skills
Following instructions
Mechanical/manipulative

Work Environment
Primarily outdoors
Primarily multiple locations

Minimum Education Level
Apprenticeship

Salary Range
$18,400 to $42,600 to $69,300

Certification or Licensing
Voluntary

Outlook
About as fast as the average

Overview

Line installers and *cable splicers* construct, maintain, and repair the vast network of wires and cables that transmit electric power, telephone, and cable television lines to commercial and residential customers. Line construction and cable splicing is a vital part of the communications system. Workers are involved in linking electricity between generation plants and homes and other buildings, merging phone communications between telephone central offices and customers, and bringing cable television stations to residences and other locations. There are approximately 279,000 line installers and cable splicers working in the United States.

History

The occupation of line installers and cable splicers is related to major developments in electromagnetic technology since the late 19th century. The roots of this technology are traced to 1831, when Michael Faraday (1791-1867) discovered electric induction. In the late 1880s came the invention and patents for the incandescent lamp, and by the turn of the century electric lighting was a common phenomenon throughout urban areas.

The generation of electricity took on further commercial significance as the telecommunications industry was born after Alexander Graham Bell's (1847-1922) patent of the telephone in 1876. During the first quarter of the 20th century, the electronics industry focused on communications and broadcast entertainment. As the need developed for more and more telephone lines to connect distant points throughout the country, line installers and cable splicers were trained and employed to construct and maintain these lines.

After World War II, the television started to become a common addition in homes around the country. In the 1950s, cable television systems were designed for better reception of network broadcasts in remote areas, and by the 1970s such systems were becoming familiar to residential viewers. Extensive construction of cable systems was begun during the 1980s to provide service to people in all geographic regions. In the 1990s, many cable television companies started to use fiber optics for new systems and to upgrade existing systems. Fiber optic technology increases network capacity, thus allowing more channels to subscribers, and allows for higher-quality sound reception.

Today, both cable television and telephone companies are using advanced technologies to modernize their equipment and build new telecommunications systems that allow voice, data, and video transmissions over the same lines. Telephone companies are building networks of cables and other equipment that will allow them to offer cable services, and cable television companies are entering the telephone business. Cox Communications, MediaOne, Cablevision, and Jones Communications are some of the cable operators offering phone service to homes and businesses in more than 25 markets. This is expected to generate increased construction activity during the 21st century; however, it is uncertain how many jobs will be generated from the expected boom, as much of the new equipment is maintenance-free and requires far fewer workers in terms of repairs and upkeep.

The Job

In the installation of new telephone and electric power lines, workers use power-driven machinery to first dig holes and erect the poles or towers that are used to support the cables. (In some areas, lines must be buried underground, and in these cases installers use power-driven equipment to dig and to place the cables in underground conduits.) These line installers, also called *outside plant technicians* and *construction line workers,* climb the poles using metal rungs (or they use truck-mounted work platforms) and install the necessary equipment and cables.

Installers who work with telephone lines usually leave the ends of the wires free for cable splicers to connect afterward; installers who work with electric power lines usually do the splicing of the wires themselves. For work on electric power lines, insulators must first be set into the poles before cables are attached. To join sections of power line and to conduct transformers and electrical accessories, line installers splice, solder, and insulate the conductors and related wiring. In some cases, line installers must attach other equipment—such as transformers, circuit breakers, and devices that deter lightning—to the line poles.

In addition to working with lines for electric power and telephones, installers set up lines for cable television transmission. Such lines carry broadcast signals from microwave towers to customer bases. Cable television lines are hung on the same poles with power and phone lines, or they are buried underground. In some cases, installers must attach other wires to the customer's premises in order to connect the outside lines to indoor television sets.

After line installers have completed the installation of underground conduits or poles, wires, and cables, cable splicers complete the line connections; they also rearrange wires when lines are changed. To join the individual wires within the cable, splicers must cut the lead sheath and insulation from the cables. They then test or phase out each conductor to identify corresponding conductors in adjoining cable sections according to electrical diagrams and specifications. At each splice, they either wrap insulation around the wires and seal the joint with a lead sleeve or cover the splice with some other type of closure. Sometimes they fill the sheathing with pressurized air so that leaks can be located and repaired.

In the past, copper was the material of choice for cables, but fiber optics are now replacing the outdated material. Fiber optic cables are hair-thin strands of glass that transmit signals more efficiently than do copper wires. For work with fiber optic cable, splicing is performed in workshop vans located near the splice area. Splicers of copper cables do their work on aerial platforms, down manholes, in basements, or in underground vaults where the cables are located.

Preventive maintenance and repair work occupy major portions of the line installer's and cable splicer's time. When wires or cables break or poles are knocked down, workers are sent immediately to make emergency repairs. Such repair work is usually necessary after the occurrence of such disasters as storms and earthquakes. The *line crew supervisor* is notified when there is a break in a line and is directed to the trouble spot by workers who keep a check on the condition of all lines in given areas. During the course of routine periodic inspection, the line installer also makes minor repairs and line changes. Workers often use electric and gas pressure tests to detect possible trouble.

To allow for the demands of high-speed, high-definition transmissions, many telecommunications companies are installing fiber optic cables. The use of hybrid fiber/coax systems requires far less maintenance than traditional copper-based networks. Line installers and cable splicers will spend significantly less time repairing broken wires and cables once hybrid fiber/coax systems become more prevalent. As the cost of fiber cables decrease and become more in line with the costs of copper cables, more cable companies will make the switch.

Included in this occupation are many specialists, such as the following: section line maintainers, tower line repairers, line construction checkers, tower erectors, and cable testers. Other types of related workers include trouble shooters, test desk trouble locators, steel-post installers, radio interference investigators, and electric powerline examiners.

Requirements

High School

You'll need math courses to prepare for the technical nature of this career. While in high school you should also take any shop classes that will teach you the principles of electricity and how to work with it. In addition, you will benefit from taking any classes that deal with electricity at a vocational or technical college in your area. Other high school shop classes, such as machinery, will give you the opportunity to work with tools and improve your hand-eye coordination. Science classes that involve lab work will also be beneficial. Take computer classes so that you will be able to use this tool in your professional life. Because you may be frequently interacting with customers, take English, speech, and other courses that will help you develop communication skills.

Postsecondary Training

Many companies prefer to hire applicants with a high school diploma or the equivalent. Although specific educational courses are not required, you'll need certain qualifications. It is helpful to have some knowledge of the basic principles of electricity and the procedures involved in line installation; such information can be obtained through attending technical programs or having been a member of the armed forces. Many employers, particularly for cable television installation, prefer to hire applicants who have received some technical training or completed a trade school or technical program that offers certification classes in technology such as fiber optics. Training can also be obtained through special classes offered through trade associations. The Society for Cable Telecommunications Engineers (SCTE) offers seminars that provide hands-on, technical training.

In many companies, entry-level employees must complete a formal apprenticeship program combining classroom instruction with supervised on-the-job training. These programs often last several years and are administered by both the employer and the union representing the employees. The programs may involve computer-assisted instruction as well as hands-on experience with simulated environments.

Certification or Licensing

SCTE also offers an Installer Certification Program. Certification is not a national requirement for employment, but the worker with certification demonstrates to employers that he or she has achieved a certain level of technical training and is qualified to perform certain functions. (The address for SCTE is listed at the end of this article.)

Employers may also give preemployment tests to applicants to determine verbal, mechanical, and mathematical aptitudes; some employers test applicants for such physical qualifications as stamina, balance, coordination, and strength. Workers who drive a company vehicle need a driver's license and a good driving record.

Many workers are represented by unions, and union membership may be required. Two unions that represent many line installers and cable splicers are the International Brotherhood of Electrical Workers and the Communications Workers of America.

Other Requirements

You'll need manual dexterity and to be in good physical shape. Much of your work will involve climbing poles and ladders, so you'll need to feel comfortable with heights. You also need to be strong in order to carry heavy equipment up poles and ladders. Also, because lines and cables are color coded, you should have the ability to distinguish such colors. You may have extensive contact with the public and need to be polite and courteous.

Exploring

In high school or vocational school, you can test your ability and interest in the occupations of line installer and cable splicer through courses in mathematics, electrical applications, and machine shop. Hobbies that involve knowledge of and experience with electricity also provide valuable practical experience. To observe line installers and cable splicers at work, it may be possible to have a school counselor arrange a field trip by calling the public relations office of the local telephone or cable television company.

Direct training and experience in telephone work may be gained in the armed forces. Frequently, those who have received such training are given preference for job openings and may be hired in positions above the entry level.

Employers

There are approximately 279,000 line installers and cable splicers working in the United States. Most work for telephone or cable television companies. They also find work with electric power companies. Some installers also work for the freelance construction companies that contract with telecommunications companies.

Starting Out

Those who meet the basic requirements and are interested in becoming either a line installer or a cable splicer may inquire about job openings by directly contacting the personnel offices of local telephone companies, utility companies, and cable television providers.

Persons enrolled in a trade school or technical institute may be able to find out about job openings through their schools' job placement services. Occasionally, employers will contact teachers and program administrators, so it is helpful to check with them also. Some positions are advertised through classified advertisements in the newspaper. Because many line installers are members of unions such as the International Brotherhood of Electrical Workers or the Communications Workers of America, job seekers can contact their local offices for job leads and assistance or visit their Web sites.

Advancement

Entry-level line installers are generally hired as helpers, trainees, or ground workers; cable splicers tend to work their way up from the position of line installer.

After successfully completing an on-the-job training program, the employee will be assigned either as a line crew member under the guidance of a line supervisor or as a cable splicer's helper under the guidance of experienced splicers. Cable splicers' helpers advance to positions of qualified cable splicers after three to four years of working experience.

Both the line installer and the cable splicer must continue to receive training throughout their careers, not only to qualify for advancement but also to keep up with the technological changes that occur in the industry. Usually it takes line installers about six years to reach top pay for their job; top pay for cable splicers is earned after about five to seven years of work experience.

Opportunities for advancement may be limited due to the declining number of positions for line installers and cable splicers. A worker may qualify for a higher level position, but may have to wait a lengthy period before an opening occurs. In companies represented by unions, opportunities for advancement may be based on seniority. Workers who demonstrate technical expertise in addition to certain personal characteristics, such as good judgment, planning skills, and the ability to deal with people, may progress to foremen or line crew supervisors. With additional training, the line installer or the cable splicer may advance to telephone installer, telephone repairer, communications equipment technician, or another higher ranked position.

Earnings

For line installers and cable splicers, earnings vary according to different regions of the country, and as with most occupations, work experience and length of service determine advances in scale. In general, however, line installers and repairers had a median hourly wage of $20.48 in 1998, according to the U.S. Department of Labor. This hourly wage translated into a yearly income of approximately $42,600. Those working only with cable line installation and repair had a median hourly wage of $15.75 in 1998, which made a yearly income of approximately $32,760. The lowest paid 10 percent of all of these workers made approximately $8.85 per hour ($18,400 per year), while the highest paid 10 percent made approximately $33.32 per hour ($69,300 per year). When emergencies arise and overtime is necessary during unscheduled hours, workers are guaranteed a minimum rate of pay that is higher than their regular rate.

Beginning workers and those with only a few years of experience make significantly less than more experienced workers. As mentioned earlier, the turnover rate in these occupations is low; therefore, many workers are in the higher wage categories. Also, cable splicers who work with fiber optics tend to earn more than those who work with copper cables.

Telephone companies often provide workers with many benefits. Although benefits vary from company to company, in general, most workers receive paid holidays, vacations, and sick leaves. In addition, most companies offer medical, dental, and life insurance plans. Some companies offer pension plans.

Work Environment

Most line installers and cable splicers work standard 40-hour weeks, though evening and weekend work is not unusual. For example, line installers and cable splicers who work for construction companies may need to schedule their work around contractors' activities and then be required to rush to complete a job on schedule. Shift work, such as four 10-hour days or working Tuesday through Saturday, is common for many workers. Most workers earn extra pay for any work over 40 hours a week.

Some workers are on call 24 hours a day and need to be available for emergencies. Both occupations require that workers perform their jobs outdoors, often in severe weather conditions when emergency repairs are needed. Construction line installers usually work in crews of two to five persons, with a supervisor directing the work of several of these crews. Work may involve extensive travel, including overnight trips during emergencies to distant locations.

There is a great deal of climbing involved in these occupations, and some underground work must be done in stooped and cramped conditions. Cable splicers sometimes perform their work on board a marine craft if they are employed with an underwater cable crew.

The work can be physically demanding and poses significant risk of injury from shocks or falls. The hazards of this work have been greatly reduced, though, by concerted efforts to establish safety standards. Such efforts have been put forward by the telephone companies, utility companies, and appropriate labor unions.

Outlook

The U.S. Department of Labor anticipates that employment growth for line installers and cable splicers will be about as fast as the average through 2008, though the trend will vary among industries. For example, for those working specifically for electric companies, job growth will see little change; while those working as telephone or cable television installers are predicted to have job growth faster than the average. There tends to be a low rate of employee turnover, but new employees will be needed to replace those who retire or leave the field.

For More Information

To learn about issues affecting jobs in telecommunications, visit the following Web site:

Communications Workers of America
501 Third Street, NW
Washington, DC 20001
Tel: 202-434-1100
Web: http://www.cwa-union.org

For information about union representation, contact:

International Brotherhood of Electrical Workers
1125 15th Street, NW
Washington, DC 20005
Tel: 202-833-7000
Web: http://www.ibew.org

For information on training seminars and certification, contact:

Society for Cable Telecommunications Engineers
140 Philips Road
Exton, PA 19341
Tel: 800-542-5040
Web: http://www.scte.org/

For information about conferences, special programs, and membership, contact:

Women in Cable and Telecommunications
230 West Monroe, Suite 2630
Chicago, IL 60606
Tel: 312-634-2330
Web: http://www.wict.org

Metallurgical Engineers

Chemistry Physics	School Subjects
Leadership/management Technical/scientific	Personal Skills
Primarily indoors One location with some travel	Work Environment
Bachelor's degree	Minimum Education Level
$38,500 to $55,000 to $85,000+	Salary Range
None available	Certification or Licensing
Little change or more slowly than the average	Outlook

Overview

Metallurgical engineers develop new types of metal alloys and adapt existing materials to new uses. They manipulate the atomic and molecular structure of materials in controlled manufacturing environments, selecting materials with desirable mechanical, electrical, magnetic, chemical, and heat-transfer properties that meet specific performance requirements.

History

Metals weren't scientifically examined until the 19th century, but the roots of the science of metallurgy were developed more than 6,000 years before that. As far back as the Stone Age, when tools and weapons were being carved from rocks, people discovered that some rocks were actually nuggets of gold and could be used as a measure of value as well as for jewelry and ornaments.

By about 4300 BC, metals were being melted and molded into usable forms such as weapons. People then discovered that metals could be improved by mixing them with other components (such as blending copper and tin to form bronze). Such mixed metals are known as alloys. Metallurgical discoveries like this helped shape the flow of human civilization. After people discovered that copper could be melted to produce bronze, tougher weapons and tools were produced, thus changing aspects of warfare and power.

Rock deposits that contained metals became valuable, and people who had access to them wielded power. Such profitable mineral rock deposits came to be known as ores, and early alchemists developed methods for finding and preparing these ore deposits for metal extraction.

Iron has been an important metal extract since about 1200 BC, the beginning of the Iron Age. Alchemists refined smelting processes and began producing brass by combining copper and zinc, which was used to make coins in the Roman Empire. Throughout the next centuries, lead, silver, and gold (among other metals) continued to be mined, but the most significant developments in metallurgy focused on applications for iron. During the 18th and 19th centuries, metallurgists began to better understand the properties of metals. It was then that metallurgy as a science began.

Physical metallurgy, as a modern science, dates back to 1890, when a group of metallurgists began the study of alloys. Enormous advances were made in the 20th century, including the development of stainless steel, the discovery of a strong but lightweight aluminum, and the increased use of magnesium and its alloys. In recent years, metallurgical scientists have extended their research into nonmetallic materials, such as ceramics, glass, plastics, and semiconductors. This field has grown so broad that it is now often referred to as "materials science" to emphasize that it deals with both metallic and nonmetallic substances.

A relatively new area of metallurgy is powder metallurgy. Scientists have developed a process in which metals are turned into powders, compressed, and then heat-treated to produce a desired product. This method has resulted in the development of new alloys and composite materials.

Metallurgists are also concentrating on ways to reclaim and recycle solid wastes in order to conserve our natural resources and protect our environment. Many mineral-rich underground deposits have been depleted. Our bridges, buildings, and machines are made with metals that today have become more difficult to mine and more scarce than ever before. Metallurgical engineers are also focusing on issues concerning environmental protection (because extraction processes create pollution), recycling methods, and more efficient, automated processes of metal recovery, production, and reuse.

The Job

Metallurgical engineers are sometimes also referred to as *metallurgists.* There are basically three categories in which such engineers work. *Extractive metallurgists,* also known as *chemical metallurgists,* are concerned with the methods used to separate metals from ores and the reclamation of materials from solid wastes for recycling. As part of their responsibilities, they may supervise and control concentrating and refining processes in commercial mining operations. They may determine the methods used to concentrate the ore by separating minerals from dirt, rock, and other unwanted materials. Many of these separation methods are performed at a treatment plant or refinery. There the extractive metallurgist may supervise and control both the separation processes and final purification processes.

Extractive metallurgists also develop ways to improve the current methods of separating minerals. To do this, the extractive metallurgist processes small batches of ores in a laboratory and analyzes the efficiency of each operation and the feasibility of adapting the operations to commercial use. Extractive metallurgists also research ways to use new sources of metals, such as the reclamation of magnesium from seawater.

Extractive metallurgists often are involved in the design of treatment plants and refineries, and the equipment and processes used within them. They may determine the types of machines needed, supervise the installation of machinery, train refinery workers, and closely observe processing operations. They monitor operations and suggest new methods and modifications needed to improve efficiency.

Because minerals are becoming depleted in the environment, extractive metallurgical engineers are constantly searching for new ways to take metals from low-grade ores and to recycle metals that are considered scrap material. During the last 20 years, many of the refining processes have greatly improved, lessening environmental damage from waste materials.

Physical metallurgists, on the other hand, focus on the scientific study of the relationship between the structure and properties of metals and devise uses for metals. These engineers begin their job after metals have been extracted and refined. At that point, most such metals are not yet useful, so they must be improved by being blended with other metals and nonmetals to produce alloys.

Physical metallurgists may conduct X-ray and microscopic experiments on the metals to determine their physical structure and other characteristics, such as the amount of alloys and base metals present. These engineers also test the materials for impurities and defects and determine whether they can be used in thermal, electrical, or magnetic applications. The results of the studies and tests determine what the metal will be used for and how long it is expected to last.

Using the data gained during research, physical metallurgists also develop new applications for metals. They devise processes that transform the metals so they have desired characteristics such as hardness, corrosion resistance, malleability, and durability. These processes include hot working, cold working, foundry methods, powder metallurgy, nuclear metallurgy, and heat treatment. After the metals have been processed, they can be transformed into commercial products. *Metallographers* conduct the laboratory investigations on metal samples and prepare reports for physical metallurgists to evaluate.

Lastly, *process metallurgical engineers*, or *mechanical metallurgical engineers*, take metals and, by melting, casting, and mechanically processing them, produce forms that will be sold for a multitude of applications, such as automotive parts, satellite components, or coins. The field of process metallurgy is quite broad, involving such methods as welding, soldering, plating, rolling, and finishing metals to produce commercially standard products.

Requirements

High School

During high school, you should pursue a strong background in mathematics and physical sciences. At the very least, take chemistry and physics as well as algebra, geometry, and trigonometry. Computer science, analytical geometry, calculus, engineering science, and design are also recommended.

Postsecondary Training

If your career goal is to become a metallurgical engineer, you will need a bachelor of science degree in materials or metallurgical engineering. Degrees are granted in many different specializations by more than 80 universities and colleges in the United States.

The first two years of college focus on subjects such as chemistry, physics, and mathematics, which are geared toward teaching analytical thinking. Students also take introductory engineering. By your sophomore year, you should have decided on a field of specialization because about one-third of your courses from then on will focus on metallurgy and related engineering areas.

There are a wide variety of programs available at colleges and universities, and it is helpful to explore as many of these programs as possible , especially those accredited by the Accreditation Board for Engineering and Technology. Some programs prepare students for practical design and production work; others concentrate on theoretical science and mathematics.

More than 50 percent of metallurgical engineers begin their first job with a bachelor's degree. Many engineers continue on for a master's degree either immediately after graduation or after a few years of work experience. A master's degree generally takes two years of study. A doctoral degree requires at least four years of study and research beyond the bachelor's degree and is usually completed by engineers interested in research or teaching at the college level.

Other Requirements

If you are interested in metallurgical engineering, you should have a curiosity about how things work, an analytical mind, and mechanical ability. In general, metallurgical engineers are interested in nature and the physical sciences, and are creative and critical thinkers who enjoy problem solving. Engineers are patient, well organized, and attentive to detail because much of their work involves long-term projects and studies. They have good communications skills and are able to explain things easily to others. In addition, they can work comfortably both alone and with other people.

Exploring

Taking sculpture and welding classes is a good way of learning the properties of metals. Creating bronze sculptures, designing and making metal jewelry, and welding metals into structures provides hands-on experience. Interested high school students should read publications like *JETS Report,* which is published by the Junior Engineering Technical Society (JETS). Science clubs such as JETS give students the opportunity to compete in academic events, take career exploration tests, and gain hands-on experience with metals and other materials.

Other excellent opportunities are found at summer camps and special academic programs. For example, Vanderbilt University has a summer program for high school students called Preparatory Academics for Vanderbilt

Engineers (PAVE). Held in Nashville, Tennessee, PAVE offers activities in engineering, computer skills, problem solving, and technical writing. In college, students may join student chapters of associations such as the Society for Mining, Metallurgy, and Exploration.

Employers

Opportunities for metallurgical engineers are found in a wide variety of settings, including metal-producing and processing companies, research institutes, and schools and universities. Engineers also work in aircraft manufacturing, machinery and electrical equipment manufacturing, the federal government, and for engineering consulting firms.

Starting Out

Most metallurgical engineers find their first job through their colleges' placement services. Technical recruiters visit universities and colleges annually to interview graduating students and possibly offer them jobs. Metallurgical engineers can also find work by directly applying to companies, through job listings at state and private employment services, or in classified advertisements in newspapers and trade publications.

Advancement

As in most occupations, the most experienced and educated workers stand the best chance for advancement. Metallurgical engineers with several years of technical experience are often eligible for supervisory positions; with further experience, engineers can apply for any number of managerial and administrative positions.

Engineers should keep current on technological advances in metallurgy throughout their careers. Many metallurgical engineers join professional associations, such as The Minerals, Metals, and Materials Society; the Society for Mining, Metallurgy, and Exploration; and the Metallurgical Society of the Canadian Institute of Mining, Metallurgy, and Petroleum. These associations hold annual conferences and meetings, in addition to other activities, which keep members up to date on recent developments and events within the industry. Special recognition through awards, scholarships, grants, and fellowships are often given to those who demonstrate outstanding achievement in the field. For example, the Application to Practice Award is presented by The Minerals, Metals, and Materials Society to individuals who excel in translating their research work into practical manufacturing applications.

Earnings

According to the U.S. Bureau of Labor Statistics, the average annual salary for metallurgical engineers is about $55,000. Those with advanced degrees and experience can earn $85,000 or more per year, while recent graduates average about $38,500 annually. Benefits vary depending on the company but usually include paid vacations and holidays, sick days, medical and dental insurance, profit sharing, and retirement plans. Some companies offer tuition assistance for continuing education and pay for membership and expenses for participation in professional associations.

Work Environment

Extractive metallurgical engineers usually work in ore treatment plants, refineries, smelter plants, or steel mills. They may also work at remote mining sites. Those working in physical metallurgy are usually located in labs or manufacturing plants, doing research and conducting studies on extracted metals. Process engineers work in a diverse range of environments, including welding shops, rolling mills, and industrial production plants for such products as automobiles and computer parts.

Those who choose research as their specialty will spend much time in labs and libraries. Those who work on school faculties will spend time in classrooms, but many are also employed by companies as working professional metallurgists.

Most metallurgical engineers work a 40-hour week. Metallurgical engineers who are employed in industrial refining may work on night shifts. Occasionally, evening or weekend work may be necessary to complete special projects or work on experiments.

Outlook

Employment for metallurgical engineers is expected to grow more slowly than the average because many of the industries in which metallurgical engineers work are expected to have little if any employment growth through 2008. However, engineers should find sufficient job openings because of the low number of new graduates relative to other engineering disciplines.

Metallurgical engineers will increasingly work with companies that are developing new methods of processing low-grade ores, that is, those that have not yet been tapped because they are not as profitable as higher grades. As the world's ore deposits become further depleted, engineers will be needed to locate new sites and devise new alloy combinations. Also, metallurgical engineers will find jobs with companies that develop new methods of recycling scrap metals and those that devise nonpolluting processing systems and cleanup methods for existing plants.

For More Information

For a list of accredited engineering programs at colleges and universities, contact:

Accreditation Board for Engineering and Technology, Inc.
111 Market Place, Suite 1050
Baltimore, MD 21202
Tel: 410-347-7700
Email: accreditation@abet.org
Web: http://www.abet.org/

For information on its summer program for high school students, contact:

Preparatory Academics for Vanderbilt Engineers
Vanderbilt University
VU Station B 351736
2301 Vanderbilt Place
Nashville, TN 37235-1736
Tel: 615-322-7827
Web: http://www.vuse.vanderbilt.edu/~pave-req/

For information on careers, educational programs, student chapters, and scholarships, contact the following organizations:

ASM International
9639 Kinsman Road
Materials Park, OH 44073-0002
Tel: 440-338-5151
Web: http://www.asm-intl.org

Junior Engineering Technical Society, Inc.
1420 King Street, Suite 405
Alexandria, VA 22314
Tel: 703-548-5387
Email: jets@nae.edu
Web: http://www.jets.org

Society for Mining, Metallurgy, and Exploration
8307 Shaffer Parkway
Littleton, CO 80127
Tel: 800-763-3132
Email: smenet@aol.com
Web: http://www.smenet.org

The Minerals, Metals, and Materials Society
184 Thorn Hill Road
Warrendale, PA 15086-7514
Tel: 724-776-9000
Email: tmsgeneral@tms.org
Web: http://www.tms.org

For online information about engineering careers, check out the following Web site:

National Engineering Information Center
Web: http://www.asee.org/neic

Nuclear Engineers

Overview

Nuclear engineers are concerned with accessing, using, and controlling the energy released when the nucleus of an atom is split. The process of splitting atoms, called fission, produces a nuclear reaction, which creates radiation in addition to nuclear energy. Nuclear energy and radiation has many uses. Some engineers design, develop, and operate nuclear power plants, which are used to generate electricity and power navy ships. Others specialize in developing nuclear weapons, medical uses for radioactive materials, and disposal facilities for radioactive waste. There are approximately 12,000 nuclear engineers employed in the United States.

History

Nuclear engineering as a formal science is quite young. However, part of its theoretical foundation rests with the ancient Greeks. In the fifth century BC, Greek philosophers postulated that the building blocks of all matter were indestructible elements, which they named *atomos,* meaning "indivisible." This atomic theory was accepted for centuries until the British chemist and physicist John Dalton (1766-1844) revised it in the early 1800s. In the following century, scientific and mathematical experimentation led to the formation of modern atomic and nuclear theory.

Today, it is known that the atom is far from indivisible and that its dense center, the nucleus, can be split to create tremendous energy. The first occurrence of this splitting process was inadvertently induced in 1938 by two German chemists. Further studies confirmed this process and established that the fragments resulting from the fission in turn strike the nuclei of other atoms, resulting in a chain reaction that produces constant energy.

The discipline of modern nuclear engineering is traced to 1942, when physicist Enrico Fermi (1901-1954) and his colleagues produced the first self-sustained nuclear chain reaction in the first nuclear reactor ever built. In 1950, North Carolina State College offered the first accredited nuclear engineering program. By 1965, nuclear engineering programs had become widely available at universities and colleges throughout the country and worldwide. These programs provided engineers with a background in reactor physics and control, heat transfer, radiation effects, and shielding.

Current applications in the discipline of nuclear engineering include the use of reactors to propel naval vessels and the production of radioisotopes for medical purposes. Most of the growth in the nuclear industry, however, has focused on the production of electric energy.

Despite the controversy over the risks involved with atomic power, in 1998 Lithuania derived 77 percent of its electricity from nuclear power; France, 76 percent; Belgium, 55 percent; Sweden, 46 percent; Korea, 41 percent; and the United States, 20 percent. Medicine, manufacturing, and agriculture have also benefited from nuclear research. Such use requires the continued development of nuclear waste management. Low-level wastes, which result from power plants as well as hospitals and research facilities, must be reduced in volume, packed in leak-proof containers, and buried, and waste sites must be continually monitored.

The Job

Nuclear engineers are involved in various aspects of the generation, use, and maintenance of nuclear energy and the safe disposal of its waste. Nuclear engineers work on research and development, design, fuel management, safety analysis, operation and testing, sales, and education. Their contributions affect consumer and industrial power supplies, medical technology, the food industry, and other industries.

Nuclear engineering is dominated by the power industry. Some engineers work for companies that manufacture reactors. They research, develop, design, manufacture, and install parts used in these facilities, such as core supports, reflectors, thermal shields, biological shields, instrumentation, and safety and control systems.

Those who are responsible for the maintenance of power plants must monitor operations efficiently and guarantee that facilities meet safety standards. Nuclear energy activities in the United States are closely supervised and regulated by government and independent agencies, especially the Nuclear Regulatory Commission (NRC). The NRC oversees the use of nuclear materials by electric utility companies throughout the United States. NRC employees are responsible for ensuring the safety of nongovernment nuclear materials and facilities and for making sure that related operations do not adversely affect public health or the environment. Nuclear engineers who work for regulatory agencies are responsible for setting the standards that all organizations involved with nuclear energy must follow. They issue licenses, establish rules, implement safety research, perform risk analyses, conduct on-site inspections, and pursue research. The NRC is one of the main regulatory agencies employing nuclear engineers.

Many nuclear engineers work directly with public electric utility companies. Tasks are diverse, and teams of engineers are responsible for supervising construction and operation, analyzing safety, managing fuel, assessing environmental impact, training personnel, managing the plant, storing spent fuel, managing waste, and analyzing economic factors.

Some engineers working for nuclear power plants focus on the quality of the water supply. Their plants extract salt from water, and engineers develop new methods and designs for such desalinization systems.

The food supply also benefits from the work of nuclear engineers. Nuclear energy is used for pasteurization and sterilization, insect pest control, and fertilizer production. Furthermore, nuclear engineers conduct genetic research on improving various food strains and their resistance to harmful elements.

Nuclear engineers in the medical field design and construct equipment for diagnosing and treating illnesses and disease. They perform research on radioisotopes, which are produced by nuclear reactions. Radioisotopes are used in heart pacemakers, X-ray equipment, and for sterilizing medical instruments. Fifty percent of all U.S. hospital patients benefit from a procedure or device that uses radioisotopes.

Numerous other jobs are performed by nuclear engineers. *Nuclear health physicists, nuclear criticality safety engineers,* and *radiation protection technicians* conduct research and training programs designed to protect plant and laboratory employees against radiation hazards. *Nuclear fuels research engineers* and *nuclear fuels reclamation engineers* work with reprocessing systems for atomic fuels. *Accelerator operators* coordinate the operation of equipment used in experiments on subatomic particles, and scanners work with photographs, produced by particle detectors, of atomic collisions.

Requirements

High School

If you are interested in becoming a professional engineer, you must begin preparing yourself in high school. You should take honors-level courses in mathematics and the sciences. Specifically, you should complete courses in algebra, geometry, trigonometry, and calculus; chemistry, physics, and biology; English, social studies, foreign language (many published technical papers that are required reading in later years are written in German or French) and humanities; and computer science.

Postsecondary Training

Professional engineers must have at least a bachelor's degree. You should attend a four-year college or university that is approved by the Accreditation Board for Engineering and Technology. In a nuclear engineering program, you will focus on subjects similar to those studied in high school but at a more advanced level. Courses also include engineering sciences and atomic and nuclear physics.

These subjects will prepare you for analyzing and designing nuclear systems and understanding how they operate. You will learn and comprehend what is involved in the interaction between radiation and matter; radiation measurements; the production and use of radioisotopes; reactor physics and engineering; and fusion reactions. The subject of safety will be emphasized, particularly with regards to handling radiation sources and implementing nuclear systems.

You must have a master's or doctoral degree for most jobs in research, higher education, and for supervisory and administrative positions. It is recommended that you obtain a graduate degree in nuclear engineering because this level of education will help you obtain the skills required for advanced specialization in the field. Many institutions that offer advanced degrees have nuclear reactors and well-equipped laboratories for teaching and research. You can obtain information about these schools by contacting the U.S. Department of Energy.

Certification or Licensing

A professional engineer license is usually required before obtaining employment on public projects (i.e., work that may affect life, health, or property). Although registration guidelines differ for each state, most states require a degree from an accredited engineering program, four years of work experience in the field, and a minimum grade on a state exam.

Other Requirements

Nuclear engineers will encounter two unique concerns. First, exposure to high levels of radiation may be hazardous; thus, engineers must always follow safety measures. Those working near radioactive materials must adhere to strict precautions outlined by regulatory standards. In addition, female engineers of childbearing age may not be allowed to work in certain areas or perform certain duties because of the potential harm to the human fetus from radiation.

Finally, nuclear engineers must be prepared for a lifetime of continuing education. Because nuclear engineering is founded in the fundamental theories of physics and the notions of atomic and nuclear theory are difficult to conceptualize except mathematically, an aptitude for physics, mathematics, and chemistry is indispensable.

Exploring

Each year, the U.S. Department of Energy (DOE) sponsors a program for high school science honor students. You are eligible for this program if you are 16 to 18 years of age and have finished the 11th grade. This program has focused on the areas of high-energy particle physics, computational sciences using the Cray II supercomputer, and materials science involving superconductivity. The DOE pays for round-trip airfare, lodging, meals, recreational activities, and special awards. If you are interested in this program, contact your school's student honors program.

If you are in the top 10 percent of your class and between 11 and 17 years of age, you are eligible for Clemson University's summer science and engineering honors program. In this program, participants conduct lab experiments and participate in field trips related to subjects such as physics, biology, and creativity in engineering design. For more information, contact the school (see the end of this article for the address).

If you are interested in becoming an engineer, you can join science clubs such as the Junior Engineering Technical Society (JETS), which has a chapter in almost every state. Science clubs provide the opportunity to work with others, design engineering projects, and participate in career exploration. Its publication, *JETS Report,* will introduce you to the organization and includes articles about club activities and student interests. If you are a more advanced student, you may want to read *ANS News,* published by the American Nuclear Society. This publication reports monthly on the society's members and activities.

Employers

Nuclear engineers work in a variety of settings. In 1998, the following three sectors each represented about 20 percent of nuclear engineers: utilities, the federal government, and engineering consulting firms. Another 12 percent were in research and testing services. More than half of all federally employed nuclear engineers were civilian employees of the navy, and most of the rest worked for the Nuclear Regulatory Commission, the Department of Energy, or the Tennessee Valley Authority. Most nonfederally employed nuclear engineers worked for public utilities or engineering consulting companies. Some worked for defense manufacturers or manufacturers of nuclear power equipment.

Starting Out

Most students begin their job search while still in college, collecting advice from job counselors and their schools' placement centers. Also, the U.S. Department of Energy has training programs that help applicants qualify for positions in nuclear engineering. For information, contact the agency's

Office of Personnel Management. The Society of Women Engineers also administers several certificate and scholarship programs and advises students regarding job placements.

As with other engineering disciplines, a hierarchy of workers exists, with the chief engineer having overall authority over managers and project engineers. This is true whether you are working in research, design, production, sales, or teaching. After gaining a certain amount of experience, engineers may apply for positions in supervision and management.

Advancement

Because the nuclear engineering field is so young, the time is ripe for technological developments, and engineers must therefore keep abreast of new research and technology throughout their careers. Advancement for engineers is contingent upon continuing education, research activity, and on-the-job expertise.

Advancement may also bring recognition in the form of grants, scholarships, fellowships, and awards. For example, the American Nuclear Society has established a Young Members Engineering Achievement Award to recognize outstanding work performed by members. To be eligible for this award, you must be younger than 40 years and demonstrate effective application of engineering knowledge that results in a concept, design, analysis method, or product used in nuclear power research and development or in a manufacturing application.

Earnings

Nuclear engineers earned a median annual salaries $71,310 in 1998, according to the U.S. Department of Labor. The highest paid 10 percent earned more than $106,400, while the lowest paid 10 percent earned less than $48,830 annually. Nuclear engineers with considerable training and experience may earn more than $120,000 a year.

Work Environment

In general, nuclear engineering is a technically demanding and politically volatile field. Those who work daily at power plants perhaps incur the most stress because they are responsible for preventing large-scale accidents involving radiation. Those who work directly with nuclear energy face risks associated with radiation contamination. Engineers handling the disposal of hazardous material also work under stressful conditions because they must take tremendous care to ensure the public's health and safety.

Research, teaching, and design occupations allow engineers to work in laboratories, classrooms, and industrial manufacturing facilities. Many engineers who are not directly involved with the physical maintenance of nuclear facilities spend most of their working hours, an average of 46 hours per week, conducting research. Most work at desks and must have the ability to concentrate on very detailed data for long periods of time, drawing up plans and constructing models of nuclear applications.

Outlook

According to the U.S. Department of Labor, the number of new jobs is expected to grow more slowly than the average for all occupations through 2008. Most openings will arise as nuclear engineers transfer to other occupations or leave the labor force. However, good opportunities for nuclear engineers should still exist because the small number of nuclear engineering graduates is likely to be in balance with the number of job openings.

An Associated Press poll conducted in March 2001 reported that 66 percent of Americans support the construction of new nuclear energy plants in the future—an increase of 24 percent since October 1999. While no new nuclear power plants are currently under construction, it is likely that the energy shortage in California and the public's growing acceptance of nuclear power will create improved employment opportunities for nuclear engineers in the near future. Even if new plants are not constructed, nuclear engineers will be needed to operate existing plants. They will also continue to be needed to work in defense-related areas, to develop nuclear medical technology, and to improve and enforce waste management and safety standards.

For More Information

For information on scholarships, education, and publications, contact:

American Nuclear Society
555 North Kensington Avenue
LaGrange Park, IL 60526
Tel: 708-352-6611
Email: outreach@ans.org
Web: http://www.ans.org

For information on its summer internship program, contact:

Clemson University
Summer Science, Engineering and Architecture Enrichment Programs
G-11 Tillman Hall, Box 345105
Clemson, SC 29634-5105
Tel: 864-656-5849
Web: http://virtual.clemson.edu/groups/summerscience/

For information on state chapters, contact:

Junior Engineering Technical Society, Inc.
1420 King Street, Suite 405
Alexandria, VA 22314
Tel: 703-548-5387
Email: jets@nae.edu
Web: http://www.jets.org

For career guidance and scholarship information, contact:

Society of Women Engineers
230 East Ohio Street, Suite 400
Chicago, IL 60611-3265
Tel: 312-644-8557
Web: http://www.swe.org

For information on honors programs, careers, and nuclear power, contact:

U.S. Department of Energy
1000 Independence Avenue, SW
Washington, DC 20585
Tel: 800-342-5363
Web: http://www.energy.gov/

Nuclear Reactor Operators and Technicians

	School Subjects
Mathematics	
Physics	

	Personal Skills
Following instructions	
Technical/scientific	

	Work Environment
Primarily indoors	
Primarily one location	

	Minimum Education Level
Some postsecondary training	

	Salary Range
$18,000 to $44,840 to $73,090+	

	Certification or Licensing
Required by all states	

	Outlook
Decline	

Overview

Nuclear reactor operator technicians enroll in formal instructional programs in preparation for becoming licensed operators. In these programs, technicians study nuclear science theory—specifically nuclear radiology; radiation detection; and reactor design, operation, and control. Technicians must also learn how to perform reactor operation and control activities in strict compliance with federally required operating and safety procedures.

For at least part of their training, nuclear reactor operator technicians work under the supervision of a licensed operator; later they work as beginning operators. They will always work under the supervision of a senior or more experienced operator.

History

The potential for nuclear power generation was first demonstrated in 1942 when a group of scientists led by Enrico Fermi (1901-1954) conducted the first controlled nuclear chain reaction in a nuclear reactor located under the football stands on Stagg Field at the University of Chicago. After World War II, research continued on peacetime uses of controlled atomic energy. in 1948, researchers increasingly emphasized the design of nuclear power reactors to generate electricity.

By late 1963, the technology for these nuclear reactors was ready for commercial use, and the first nuclear power plants were constructed. Their successful operation and the low cost of the electric power they generated were promising. Further development of technology continued, and the construction of several additional nuclear power plants began.

Since then, the field has learned a great deal about the design and safe operation of nuclear-fueled electric power plants. Quality assurance and control procedures have been developed to ensure that every step of a plant's construction and operation meets the necessary safety requirements.

Specific procedures are in place to protect against radiation, and special technicians work in each plant to ensure the least possible risk of radiation exposure to workers. Studies show that the safest operation of nuclear plants is directly attributable to carefully selected and thoroughly trained nuclear reactor operators. Since 1963, thousands of people have been trained and licensed by the federal government to work as nuclear reactor operators.

The Job

Technicians are trained to learn and perform all the duties expected of licensed operators. Almost all the skills and knowledge, however, are learned outside of the reactor control room.

The nuclear reactor is like an engine providing power, in the form of hot steam, to run the entire nuclear power plant. *Nuclear reactor operators* are the nuclear station's driver, in the sense that they control all the machines used to generate power at the station. Working under the direction of a plant manager, the nuclear reactor operator is responsible for the continuous and safe operation of a reactor. Although most nuclear power plants contain more than one nuclear reactor unit, each nuclear reactor operator is responsible for only one of the units.

From the standpoint of safety and uninterrupted operation, the nuclear reactor operator holds the most critical job in the plant. The operator's performance is considered so essential that any shutdown of an average 1,000-megawatt plant, whether due to an accident or operating error, can result in a minimal loss of the cost of the operator's salary for 10 years.

Licensed nuclear reactor operators work in the station control room, monitoring meters and gauges. They read and interpret instruments that record the performance of every valve, pump, compressor, switch, and water treatment system in the reactor unit. When necessary, they make adjustments to fission rate, pressure, water temperature, and the flow rate of the various pieces of equipment to ensure safe and efficient operation.

During each 24-hour period, operators make rounds four times. This task involves reviewing the unit's control board and writing down the parameters of the instruments. Each hour, a computer generates a reading indicating the amount of power the unit is generating.

In addition to monitoring the instruments in the control room, the nuclear reactor operator runs periodic tests, including pressure readings, flow readings, and vibration analyses on each piece of equipment. The operator must also perform logic testing on the electrical components in order to check the built-in safeguards.

Every 12 to 18 months, the nuclear reactor operator must also refuel the reactor unit, a procedure that is sometimes called an outage. During the refueling, the turbine is brought offline, or shut down. After it cools and depressurizes, the unit is opened, and any repairs, testing, and preventive maintenance are taken care of. Depleted nuclear fuel is exchanged for new fuel. The unit is then repressurized, reheated, and brought back online, or restarted.

Auxiliary equipment operators normally work at the site of the equipment. Their work can include anything from turning a valve to bringing a piece of equipment in and out of service. All of their requests for action on any of the machines must be approved by the nuclear reactor operator.

Precise operation is required in nuclear power plants to be sure that radiation does not contaminate the equipment, the operating personnel, or the nearby population and environment. The most serious danger is the release of large amounts of atomic radiation into the atmosphere. Operating personnel are directly involved in the prevention of reactor accidents and in the containment of radioactivity in the event of an accident.

Prospective nuclear reactor operators always begin employment as a technician. In this capacity, they gain plant experience and technical knowledge at a functioning nuclear power plant. The technician trains on a simulator and studies the reactor and control room. A simulator is built and equipped like an operating reactor control station. Technicians can practice operating the reactor and learn what readings the instruments in the simulator give when certain adjustments are made in the reactor control settings.

This company-sponsored training is provided to help technicians attain the expertise necessary to obtain an operator's license. Even after obtaining a license, however, beginning operators work under the direction of a shift supervisor, senior operator, or other management personnel.

Requirements

Although a college degree is not required, many utilities prefer candidates to have some postsecondary training. More and more nuclear reactor operators have completed at least two years of college, and about 25 percent have a four-year degree. Lack of college experience, however, does not exclude an applicant from being hired. High school graduates are selected based on subjects studied and aptitude test results.

High School

If you wish to enter nuclear technology programs, you should study algebra, geometry, English composition, blueprint reading, and chemistry and physics with laboratory study. In addition, classes in computer science and beginning electronics will help you prepare for the technology program that follows high school.

Postsecondary Training

In the first year of a nuclear technology program at a technical or community college, you will probably take nuclear technology, radiation physics, applied mathematics, electricity and electronics, technical communications, basic industrial economics, radiation detection and measurement, inorganic chemistry, radiation protection, mathematics, basic mechanics, quality assurance and quality control, principles of process instrumentation, heat transfer and fluid flow, metallurgy, and metal properties.

In the second year, you may be required to take technical writing and reporting, nuclear systems, blueprint reading, mechanical component characteristics and specifications, reactor physics, reactor safety, power plant systems, instrumentation and control of reactors and plant systems, power plant chemistry, reactor operations, reactor auxiliary systems, and industrial organizations and institutions.

Upon completing a technical program, you will continue training once you are employed at a plant. On-the-job training includes learning nuclear science theory; radiation detection; and reactor design, operation, and control. In addition, nuclear reactor operator technicians must learn in detail how the nuclear power plant works. Trainees are assigned to a series of work-learn tasks that take them to all parts of the plant. If trainees have been working in the plant as regular employees, their individual training is planned around what they already know. This kind of training usually takes two to three years and includes simulator practice.

The simulator is an exact replica of the station's real control room. The controls in the simulator are connected to an interactive computer. Working under the supervision of a licensed nuclear reactor operator, trainees experience mock events in the simulator, which teach them how to safely handle emergencies.

During this on-the-job training, technicians learn about nuclear power plant materials, processes, material balances, plant operating equipment, pipe systems, electrical systems, and process control. It is crucial to understand how each activity within the unit affects other instruments or systems. Nuclear reactor operator technicians are given written and oral exams, sometimes as often as once a week. In some companies, technicians are dismissed from their job for failing to pass any one training exam.

Some people in the industry believe that one of the most difficult aspects of becoming a nuclear reactor operator is getting hired. Because electric utilities invest a substantial amount of time and money to train nuclear reactor operators, they are extremely selective when hiring.

The application process entails intensive screening, including identity checks, FBI fingerprint checks, drug and alcohol tests, psychological tests, and credit checks. After passing this initial screening, the applicant takes a range of mathematical and science aptitude tests.

Utility companies recruit most nuclear reactor operator technicians from local high schools and colleges, fossil fuel plants (utilities using nonnuclear sources of energy), and nuclear navy programs. Knowledge of nuclear science and the discipline and professionalism gained from navy experience make veterans excellent candidates. Graduates of two-year programs in nuclear technology also make excellent trainees because they are well versed in nuclear and power plant fundamentals.

The standards and course content for all nuclear training programs are established by the Nuclear Regulatory Commission (NRC). In addition, each nuclear power plant training program must be accredited by the Institute of Nuclear Power Operations, which was founded in 1979 by industry leaders to promote excellence in nuclear plant operations.

Certification or Licensing

Nuclear reactor operators are required to be licensed, based on examinations given by the NRC. The licensing exam consists of three parts: a written test, usually lasting one day; an oral exam, lasting about half a day; and an actual demonstration. According to the NRC, approximately 90 percent of candidates pass the exam the first time.

The nuclear reactor operator license is issued for a six-year period and may be renewed after passing a requalification exam. The license is valid for the specific power plant and a specific unit only.

Nuclear reactor operators who fail the relicensing exam are provided remedial training to improve knowledge in weak areas. The test may then be retaken in six months. In addition to the requalification exam, nuclear reactor operators must take an annual operating test given by the nuclear station and a written test every two years.

Other Requirements

Nuclear reactor operators are subject to continuous exams. They must attend classes and spend more than 70 hours each year training in the simulator as part of their rotating work schedule.

Because of the dangerous nature of nuclear energy, the nuclear reactor operator's performance is critical to the safety of other employees, the community, and the environment. Operators must perform their job with a high degree of precision and accuracy. They must be able to remain calm under pressure and maintain sound judgment in emergencies.

Although nuclear reactor operators must frequently perform numerous tasks at once, they must also be able to remain alert during quiet times and handle the monotony of routine readings and tests.

Responding to requests from other personnel, such as the auxiliary operators, is a regular part of the nuclear reactor operator's job. The ability to communicate and work well with other team members and plant personnel is essential.

Exploring

High school guidance counselors and advisors at community or technical colleges are good sources of information about a career as a nuclear reactor operator. The librarians in these institutions also may be helpful in directing students to introductory literature on nuclear reactors.

Opportunities for exploring a career as a nuclear reactor operator are limited because nuclear power plants are usually located in places relatively far from schools and have strictly limited visiting policies. Very few commercial or research reactors provide tours for the general public. However, many utility companies with nuclear power plants have visitors' centers, where tours are scheduled at specified hours. In addition, interested high school students usually can arrange visits to nonnuclear power plants, which allows them to learn about the energy-conversion process common to all steam-powered electric power generation plants.

Employers

In 2001, there were 103 nuclear power units in operation at over 60 sites in the United States. Thirty-one foreign countries operated about 435 nuclear power plants; 38 new nuclear plants were under construction in 13 countries.

Starting Out

In recent years, nuclear technology programs have been the best source for hiring nuclear reactor operator technicians. Students are usually interviewed and hired by the nuclear power plant personnel recruiters toward the end of their technical college program and start working in the power plant as trainees after they graduate.

Navy veterans from nuclear programs and employees from other parts of the nuclear power plant may also be good candidates for entering a nuclear reactor operator training program.

Occupational Safety and Health Workers

	School Subjects
Biology Chemistry Mathematics	
	Personal Skills
Helping/teaching Technical/scientific	
	Work Environment
Primarily indoors Primarily multiple locations	
	Minimum Education Level
Bachelor's degree	
	Salary Range
$25,500 to $60,000 to $75,000+	
	Certification or Licensing
Required for certain positions	
	Outlook
About as fast as the average	

Overview

Occupational safety and health workers are responsible for the prevention of work-related accidents and diseases, injuries from unsafe products and practices, property losses from accidents and fires, and adverse effects of industrial processes on the environment.

History

For thousands of years, people thought that accidents and illnesses just happened, or they blamed such unfortunate occurrences on fate, the wrath of the gods, or evil forces. Very little was done to prevent accidents systematically other than to wear charms, offer sacrifices, or engage in other rituals or behaviors thought to be preventative. At the same time, slave trade reinforced the concept that certain workers' lives were expendable. The builders of the great ancient structures, such as the pyramids of Egypt, gave no thought to the well-being of their human inventory other than giving them enough food so that they were strong enough to work.

Throughout history many types of workers have been compelled to accept their lot in life. Even in more modern times, the early history of the Industrial Revolution demonstrated that workers were considered less important than the machines they operated or the output of a factory or mine. Little relationship was seen between productivity and the safety and health of the workers.

These exploitative practices were eventually halted through the joint efforts of social reform movements, labor unions, and progressive politicians. The rapid growth of technology in the 20th century made it possible to design machinery and equipment with built-in safety mechanisms. As medical research increased our knowledge of the effect of the working environment on health, psychological studies made us aware of the human factors that may lead to accident or illness. Labor unions and the federal government increased the pressure on companies to pay more attention to workplace conditions and the welfare of workers.

Now in the 21st century, we are probably safer at work than in most other places, including the home. Companies of all sizes have instituted practical safety measures and reduced worker hazards by developing new machinery and devising better safeguards. At the same time, they have established work safety rules and safety education programs for their workers. To protect the well-being and productivity of their workers, companies continue to allocate large sums to research and development in this area.

The Job

Safety and health workers have a variety of responsibilities, which fall into four basic areas.

First, they identify and evaluate hazardous conditions and practices. They inspect facilities and equipment, conduct accident investigations, analyze work procedures, study building layouts, and consult with workers who are exposed to hazardous conditions.

Second, safety and health workers develop ways to control hazards. They observe, analyze, and solve problems using deductive reasoning and creativity.

Third, safety personnel communicate hazard-control information to workers and management

Fourth, safety personnel continually measure hazard-control systems and adjust them as needed. Safety employees gather information from accident investigations, inspections, customer or employee complaints, and other sources, such as government agencies and regulations. They may employ such strategies as designing or redesigning equipment and machinery, providing physical safeguards (for example, protective clothing or rock deflectors on lawn mowers), or training workers in the use of safe procedures.

Safety engineers are primarily concerned with preventing accidents. In a large industrial plant, they may develop a safety program that covers several thousand employees. They examine plans for new machinery and equipment to see that all safety precautions have been included and put in place. They determine the weight-bearing capacity of the plant floor. They inspect existing machinery and design, build, and install safeguards where necessary. Many safety engineers work with design engineers to develop safe models of their company's products and monitor the manufacturing process to make sure the finished product is safe and reliable to use.

If an accident occurs, safety engineers investigate the cause. If the accident is related to a mechanical problem, they use their technical skills to correct it and prevent a recurrence. If it is because of human error, they may educate the particular workers in proper safety procedures and draw up an education program for the entire staff.

Safety engineers who work for trucking companies are known as *safety coordinators*. They work with both management and drivers to reduce losses due to accidents. They instruct truck-and-trailer drivers in matters pertaining to traffic and safety regulations and care of the equipment. They ride with drivers and patrol highways to detect errors in handling cargo and driving the vehicle. They also watch for any violations of company regulations and observe the conditions of the vehicles and the roads. They investigate accidents and recommend measures to improve safety records and lengthen the life of equipment.

Occupational safety and health inspectors work for government and regulatory agencies. They visit workplaces to detect unsafe machinery and equipment or to check for unhealthy working conditions. They discuss their findings with the employer or plant manager and request immediate correction of violations in accordance with federal, state, and local government standards and regulations.

In the mining industry, *mining inspectors* inspect underground and open-pit mines to ensure compliance with health and safety laws. They check timber supports, electrical and mechanical equipment, storage of explosives, and other possible hazards. They test the air for toxic or explosive gas or dust. They may also design safety devices and protective equipment for mine workers, lead rescue activities in the event of an emergency, and instruct mine workers in safety and first-aid procedures.

The light, heat, and power industry employs safety engineers (known as *safety inspectors*) to ensure the safety of the workers who construct and maintain overhead and underground power lines. Safety inspectors check safety belts, ladders, ropes, and tools; observe crews at work to make sure they use goggles, rubber gloves, and other safety devices; and examine the condition of tunnels and ditches. They investigate accidents, devise preventive measures, and instruct workers in safety matters.

Fire protection engineers have different tasks depending on where they work. In general, their job is to safeguard life and property against fire, explosion, and related hazards. Those employed by design and consulting firms work with architects and other engineers to build fire safety into new buildings. They study buildings before and after completion for such factors as fire resistance, the use and contents of the buildings, water supplies, and entrance and exit facilities. Fire protection engineers who work for manufacturers of fire equipment design alarm systems, fire-detection mechanisms, and fire-extinguishing devices and systems. They also investigate causes of accidental fires and may organize and train personnel to carry out fire-protection programs.

Fire prevention research engineers conduct research to determine the causes of fires and methods for preventing them. They study such problems as fires in high-rise buildings, and they test fire retardants and the fire safety of building materials. The results of such research are then used by fire protection engineers in the field. Fire prevention research engineers also prepare educational materials on fire prevention for insurance companies.

Fire marshals supervise and coordinate the activities of the firefighters in large industrial establishments such as refineries and auto plants. They also inspect equipment such as sprinklers and extinguishers; inspect the premises for combustion hazards and violations of fire ordinances; conduct fire drills; and direct fire-fighting and rescue activities in case of emergencies.

While *safety and fire prevention engineers* work to prevent accidents, *industrial hygienists* are concerned with the health of the employees in the workplace. They collect and analyze samples of dust, gases, vapors, and other potentially toxic material; investigate the adequacy of ventilation, exhaust equipment, lighting, and other conditions that may affect employee health, comfort, or efficiency; evaluate workers' exposure to radiation and to noise; and recommend ways of controlling or eliminating such hazards. These hygienists work at the job site.

Other industrial hygienists work in the private laboratories of insurance, industrial, or consulting companies, where they analyze air samples, research health equipment, or investigate the effects of chemicals. *Health physicists* are specialists in radiation. Still other industrial hygienists specialize in the problems of air and water pollution.

Environmental safety and health workers prevent hazards to the environment and are concerned with pollution control, energy efficiency, recycling, waste disposal, and compliance with the government's Environmental Protection Agency requirements.

Loss-control and occupational health consultants are safety inspectors hired by property-liability insurance companies to perform services for their clients. They inspect insured properties and evaluate the physical conditions, safety practices, and hazardous situations that may exist; determine whether the client is an acceptable risk; calculate the amount of the insurance premium; and develop and monitor a program to eliminate or reduce all hazards. They also help set up health programs and medical services and train safety personnel.

Requirements

High School

If you are interested in becoming a occupational safety and health worker, you will need to acquire a bachelor's degree at the minimum. Therefore, while you are in high school, take a college preparatory course of study. Subjects that you should concentrate on include mathematics and sciences. Especially important are algebra, trigonometry, calculus, biology, chemistry, and physics. Because this work is so involved with people and their reactions to environments, you may also want to take psychology courses. Finally, because part of your work will include writing reports, giving presentations, and explaining changes to others, you will need to develop both your oral and written communication skills. To do this, take English classes throughout your high school years. If your school offers speech classes, you may want to take these as well.

Postsecondary Training

For your postsecondary education, you should plan on getting a bachelor's degree in engineering or in one of the physical or biological sciences. Employers usually prefer to hire a candidate with a bachelor's or master's degree that is specifically related to occupational safety and health, such as safety engineering or management, industrial hygiene, fire-protection engineering, public health, or health physics. Degrees in chemical or mechanical engineering are also very desirable. According to the American Society of Safety Engineers (ASSE), more than 125 colleges and universities offer degrees in safety management, occupational safety, environmental protection, or a related field. You can contact the Member Services Department of the society for a listing of these schools (see the end of this article for contact information). In addition to the schools offering safety degrees, some engineering schools offer a safety specialty within their traditional engineering degree programs. Many schools with safety-degree programs are having difficulty accommodating the growing interest in an occupational safety education and have long waiting lists of students. These schools, however, have no trouble placing their graduates in jobs. The ASSE and some private foundations offer scholarships.

Employers are increasingly interested in hiring people who have a knowledge of the three major categories in occupational safety and health: safety, industrial hygiene, and environmental management. Therefore, you should try to combine your studies; for example, if you major in safety, then you should minor in environmental affairs, or vice versa.

Workers in this field must keep abreast of new and changing trends and technologies. For this reason, many insurance companies provide training seminars and correspondence courses for the members of their staff. The Occupational Safety and Health Administration offers courses on topics such as occupational injury investigation and radiological health hazards. The ASSE, the National Safety Council, and other groups also provide continuing professional education for safety engineers.

In some cases you may be able to find employment with only a two-year degree, working as a safety and health technician. To advance in the field, however, you will need to complete further education.

Certification or Licensing

Certification is offered by a number of professional organizations. Requirements typically include graduation from an accredited program, a certain amount of work experience, and passing a written exam. The Board of Certified Safety Professionals (BCSP) reported that 60 percent of the employers advertising job openings in the magazine *Professional Safety* in 1999 either wanted or required job candidates to have the designation Certified Safety Professional (CSP). In addition to offering the CSP designation, the BCSP also offers certification in three speciality areas: Construction Safety, Ergonomics, and System Safety. Other organizations offering certification include the American Board of Industrial Hygiene, the National Safety Council, and the National Fire Protection Association.

States require licensure for some occupational safety and health workers, depending on the job they do. For example, professional engineers must be licensed, although exact requirements may vary from state to state. In general, however, requirements include graduation from an accredited program, work experience, and the passing of written exams.

Other Requirements

You may need to be in good physical condition to keep up with the physical demands of some of the jobs in this field. To be effective in establishing safety programs and procedures, you must be able to communicate well and motivate others. You must be adaptable and able to work comfortably with people on all levels—from union representatives to supervisors of a welding shop to corporate executives or government bureaucrats.

Exploring

Your science teachers, teachers of technical subjects, and school vocational counselors may offer guidance to useful courses of study and any available work-study programs. Math and science clubs may develop your interest in a safety career; debate teams and drama clubs can help you develop communication skills.

You may be able to interview with and attend lectures by occupational safety and health professionals, giving you an opportunity to ask questions and get an overview of the field. Field trips to an industrial plant or other worksite will also give you an appreciation for the profession.

There are no shortcuts in the educational process, but as you begin to fulfill your academic goals, you may seek part-time and summer jobs that are related to your career objectives. These jobs in turn may lead to permanent positions upon graduation. Part-time and summer jobs in manufacturing plants will give you firsthand experience in observing working conditions and help you become familiar with some of the equipment that is important to safety workers. You may also be able to find safety- or health-related jobs in local hospitals and insurance companies. Student internships are a good way to enter the field. One of the best-known internship programs is run by the Safety Studies Department at the University of Wisconsin-Whitewater (see address at the end of this article).

Another way to study the field is to check out some Web sites, such as the Occupational Safety and Health Administration site (http://www.osha.gov), WorkCare's site (http://www.osh.net), and Product Safety International's site Safety Link (http://www.safetylink.com).

Employers

Occupational safety and health workers are employed throughout the country, but they are generally concentrated in urban and industrial centers. According to the Board of Certified Safety Professionals, the fields of manufacturing, insurance, petrochemicals, consulting, and government are the largest employers of certified workers. Many of those employed in the safety and health field are safety engineers, fire protection engineers, industrial hygienists, or workers who combine two or more areas. A small number work as engineering or industrial hygiene technicians. Insurance consultants usually have their offices in one city and travel to and from various sites.

Starting Out

College guidance counselors and placement offices are one source of job leads. People intent on entering the occupational safety and health field may contact the American Society of Safety Engineers or other professional societies, talk to company recruiters, or apply directly to the personnel or employment offices of appropriate industrial or insurance companies. Safety-industry trade journals and society Web sites are also excellent sources to check for listings of job openings.

Advancement

Advancement will depend on such factors as a person's education level, area of specialty, experience, and certifications. Safety and health workers in the insurance industry, for example, may be promoted to department manager of a small branch office, then to a larger branch office, and from there to an executive position in the home office. In industrial firms, safety and health workers can move up to safety and health managers for one or more plants. Some working in the consulting area will have the advancement goal of opening their own consulting firm. Safety and health workers who obtain advanced degrees in areas such as public health or safety studies may go into teaching or move into research. Because occupational safety and health workers are so involved with businesses and government, many develop an interest in these fields and add to their credentials by getting a master's in business administration degree or a law degree. They may then go into law, administration, or various aspects of business operations. Technicians with the proper education and experience can advance to professional safety and health positions, with the accompanying increase in prestige and income.

Earnings

Earnings, naturally, vary based on factors such as the field the safety and health worker is involved in, his or her experience, and the size of the employer. The U.S. Department of Labor reported the following as 1999 salary averages for safety and health workers employed in several areas by the federal government: mine safety and health inspectors, $58,000; safety and occupational health managers, $54,000; and consumer safety inspectors, $37,300. The department also reported that safety inspectors working for the federal government had starting salaries of $25,500 to $31,200 in 1999. Government workers generally earn less than their counterparts in the private sector. According to the Board of Certified Safety Professionals, salaries for safety workers may range from approximately $30,000 to $150,000 or more. The average salaries for mid-career professionals with bachelor's or master's degrees range from approximately $60,000 to $75,000. Those with certification typically earn higher salaries.

Those who work full-time for one company usually receive health benefits and paid vacation. Consultants or self-employed workers choose their own hours and clients, but do not usually have benefits, such as insurance or paid vacation time.

Work Environment

Most occupational safety and health workers are based in offices but spend much of their time at worksites, inspecting safety hazards, talking to workers, or taking samples of such things as air, dust, or water. They may travel a great deal, depending on their job specialty and location. For example, safety engineers who work exclusively at one plant may only travel to an occasional seminar or conference, while insurance consultants will spend about half their time away from the office inspecting worksites.

The conditions of inspection sites vary depending on the situation. Safety and health workers may experience unpleasant or dangerous working conditions, such as inspecting mines or livestock-slaughtering procedures. Some factories will be dirty and noisy, while warehouses are usually orderly and office buildings very comfortable. The nature of the work may require a lot of physical activity, such as walking, stooping, bending, and lifting.

Outlook

According to the U.S. Department of Labor, inspectors and compliance officers (a category that includes a number of safety and health workers) is expected to have employment growth that is about as fast as the average through 2008. Because of wide public support, the economy seldom affects safety jobs, especially in heavy industry where exposure to injury is highest. The expansion of regulatory and compliance programs will increase opportunities in government jobs. In the private sector, employment of safety and health workers is expected to grow because of increasing self-enforcement of government and company regulations. Casualty insurance companies will hire more safety and health workers as small companies request the services of their loss-control and occupational health consultants. Openings will also occur as experienced workers move to other occupations, retire, or are promoted. Employment prospects will be best for college graduates with degrees specifically related to occupational safety or health.

One of the fastest-growing areas of safety work is with robotics. The trend toward automation has created a need for safety professionals who can understand electromechanical systems and make sure they meet safety standards. Another growing area is product safety. As more complicated consumer products are marketed to a public that is increasingly aware of safety issues, safety experts will find more opportunities in this field. Other future hotbeds of employment for qualified safety professionals include construction, petrochemicals, the semiconductor industry, multinational corporations, insurance, and meatpacking.

There is an increasing interest among employers in hiring one expert who fulfills the three functions of safety, industrial hygiene, and environmental management. Other in-demand specialties include risk management/loss control, ergonomics and human factors engineering, analytical-process safety engineering, construction safety, environmental safety, and fire protection.

For More Information

For information on certification, continuing education, and publications, contact the following organizations:

American Board of Industrial Hygiene
6015 West St. Joseph, Suite 102
Lansing, MI 48917-3980
Tel: 517-321-2638
Email: abih@abih.org
Web: http://www.abih.org

American Industrial Hygiene Association
2700 Prosperity Avenue, Suite 250
Fairfax, VA 22031
Tel: 703-849-8888
Web: http://www.aiha.org

American Society of Safety Engineers
1800 East Oakton Street
Des Plaines, IL 60018
Tel: 847-699-2929
Web: http://www.asse.org

Board of Certified Safety Professionals
208 Burwash Avenue
Savoy, IL 61874
Tel: 217-359-9263
Email: bcsp@bcsp.com
Web: http://www.bcsp.com

National Fire Protection Association
PO Box 9101
1 Batterymarch Park
Quincy, MA 02269-9101
Tel: 617-770-3000
Web: http://www.nfpa.org

National Safety Council
1121 Spring Lake Drive
Itasca, IL 60143-3201
Tel: 630-285-1121
Web: http://www.nsc.org

For the free booklet, Careers in Fire Protection Engineering, *check out the following Web site or contact:*

Society of Fire Protection Engineers
7315 Wisconsin Avenue, Suite 1225 W
Bethesda, MD 20814
Tel: 301-718-2910
Web: http://www.sfpe.org

For information about the Safety Studies program, contact:

University of Wisconsin-Whitewater
Safety Studies Department
Winther 6034
Whitewater, WI 53190
Tel: 262-472-1117
Email: safety@mail.uww.edu
Web: http://www.uww.edu/factsheets/safety.html

Operating Engineers

School Subjects
Mathematics
Technical/shop

Personal Skills
Following instructions
Mechanical/manipulative

Work Environment
Primarily outdoors
Primarily multiple locations

Minimum Education Level
Some postsecondary education

Salary Range
$15,410 to $23,360 to $37,670

Certification or Licensing
None available

Outlook
Little change or more slowly
than the average

Overview

Operating engineers operate various types of power-driven construction machines such as shovels, cranes, tractors, bulldozers, pile drivers, concrete mixers, and pumps. There are approximately 808,000 operating engineers employed in the United States.

History

The ancient Egyptians used some type of hoisting system to move the giant stone blocks of the pyramids into place. The Romans constructed roads, viaducts, and bridges, many of which are still in use today. The Great Wall of China, begun in the third century BC, remains an amazing architectural feat and is one of the few manmade structures visible from space.

These ancient marvels are even more amazing when one considers that they were all built using only human muscle and simple machines such as levers and pulleys. It was not until the Industrial Revolution and the invention of the steam engine that complex machines were extensively used in construction. After the harnessing of steam power, Western Europe and America made rapid progress in constructing buildings, roads, and water and sewerage systems.

Construction has always played an important role in societies. Today, many people measure progress by the increase in new construction in a town or city. All sizes and shapes of construction machinery have been introduced in recent years, and operating engineers work hard to stay current in their training and abilities.

The Job

Operating engineers work for a variety of construction companies as well as manufacturers and state agencies. Whatever the employer, operating engineers run power shovels, cranes, derricks, hoists, pile drivers, concrete mixers, paving machines, trench excavators, bulldozers, tractors, and pumps. They use these machines to move construction materials, earth, logs, coal, grain, and other material. Generally, operating engineers move the materials over short distances: around a construction site, factory, or warehouse or on and off trucks and ships. They also do minor repairs on the equipment, as well as keep them fueled and lubricated. They often are identified by the machines they operate.

Bulldozer operators operate the familiar bulldozer, a tractor-like vehicle with a large blade across the front for moving rocks, trees, earth, and other obstacles from construction sites. They also operate trench excavators, road graders, and similar equipment.

Crane and tower operators lift and move materials, machinery, or other heavy objects with mechanical booms and tower and cable equipment. Although some cranes are used on construction sites, most are used in manufacturing and other industries.

Excavation and loading machine operators handle machinery equipped with scoops, shovels, or buckets to excavate earth at construction sites and to load and move loose materials, mainly in the construction and mining industries.

Hoist and winch operators lift and pull heavy loads using power-operated equipment. Most work in loading operations in construction, manufacturing, logging, transportation, public utilities, and mining.

Operating engineers use various pedals, levers, and switches to run their machinery. For example, crane operators may rotate a crane on its chassis, lift and lower its boom, or lift and lower the load. They also use various attachments to the boom such as buckets, pile drivers, or heavy wrecking balls. When a tall building is being constructed, the crane and its operator may be positioned several hundred feet off the ground.

Operating engineers must have very precise knowledge about the capabilities and limitations of the machines they operate. To avoid tipping over their cranes or damaging their loads, crane operators must be able to judge distance and height and estimate their load size. They must be able to raise and lower the loads with great accuracy. Sometimes operators cannot see the point where the load is to be picked up or delivered. At these times, they follow the directions of other workers using hand or flag signals or radio transmissions.

The range of skills of the operating engineer is broader than in most building trades as the machines themselves differ in the ways they operate and the jobs they do. Some operators know how to work several types of machines, while others specialize with one machine.

Requirements

High School

A high school education or its equivalent is valuable for the operating engineer and is a requirement for apprenticeship training. Mathematics, physics, and shop classes can provide useful preparation for operating construction equipment.

Postsecondary Training

There are two ways to become an operating engineer: through a union apprentice program or on-the-job training. The apprenticeship, which lasts three years, has at least two advantages: the instruction is more complete, which results in greater employment opportunities, and both labor and management know that the apprentice is training to be a machine operator. Applicants to an apprenticeship program generally must be between the ages of 18 and 30.

Besides learning on the job, the apprentice also receives some classroom instruction in grade-plans reading, elements of electricity, physics, welding, and lubrication services. Despite the advantages of apprenticeships, most apprenticeship programs are difficult to enter because the number of apprentices is limited to the number of skilled workers already in the field.

Other Requirements

Operating engineers must have excellent mechanical aptitude and skillful coordination of eye, hand, and foot movements. In addition, because reckless use of the machinery may be dangerous to other workers, it is necessary to have a good sense of responsibility and seriousness on the job.

Operating engineers should be healthy and strong. They need the temperament to withstand dirt and noise and endure all kinds of weather conditions. Many operating engineers belong to the International Union of Operating Engineers.

Exploring

You may be able to gain practical experience of operating machines by observing them in action by working as a laborer or machine operator's helper in construction job during the summer. Such jobs may be available on local, state, and federal highway and building construction programs.

Employers

Operating engineers work for contractors who build highways, dams, airports, skyscrapers, buildings, and other large-scale projects. They also work for utilities companies, manufacturers, factories, mines, steel mills, and other firms that do their own construction work. Many work for state and local public works and highway departments.

Starting Out

Once apprentices complete their training and become journeymen, their names are put on a list; as positions open up, they are filled in order from the list of available workers. People who do not complete an apprenticeship program may apply directly to manufacturers, utilities, or contractors who employ operating engineers for entry-level jobs as machine operator's helpers.

Advancement

Some operating engineers—generally those with above-average ability and interest, as well as good working habits—advance to job supervisor and occasionally construction supervisor. Some are able to qualify for higher pay by training themselves to operate more complicated machines.

Earnings

The median annual salary for all operating engineers was about $23,360 in 1998, according to the *Occupational Outlook Handbook*. Salaries ranged from $15,410 to $37,670 a year. Rates vary according to the area of the country and the type of machine being operated. Crane and tower operators earned a median annual salary of $30,510; excavation and loading machine operators, $27,090; and hoist and winch operators, $28,030. Other factors affecting wages are the experience of the operator and purpose for which the machine is being used.

Work Environment

Operating engineers consider dirt and noise a part of their jobs. Some of the machines on which they work constantly shake and jolt them. This constant movement, along with the strenuous, outdoor nature of the work, makes this a physically tiring job. Since the work is done almost entirely outdoors in almost any kind of weather, operating engineers must be willing to work under conditions that are often unpleasant.

Outlook

Employment of all operating engineers is projected to grow more slowly than the average through 2008. This is due in part to the increased efficiency brought about by automation. Factories and plants are increasingly relying on computer-controlled material handling systems, many of which do not require a human operator.

About 75 percent of the operating engineers work in construction and local government: industries that are associated with the construction and repair of highways, bridges, dams, harbors, airports, subways, water and sewage systems, power plants, and transmission lines. Construction of schools, office and other commercial buildings, and residential property will also stimulate demand for these workers. However, the construction industry is very sensitive to changes in the overall economy, so the number of openings may fluctuate from year to year.

For More Information

For additional information, contact the following organizations:

Associated General Contractors of America
333 John Carlyle Street, Suite 200
Alexandria, VA 22314
Tel: 703-548-3118
Email: info@agc.org
Web: http://www.agc.org

International Union of Operating Engineers
1125 17th Street, NW
Washington, DC 20036
Tel: 202-429-9100
Web: http://www.iuoe.org

Petroleum Engineers

Overview

Petroleum engineers apply the principles of geology, physics, and the engineering sciences to the recovery, development, and processing of petroleum. As soon as an exploration team has located an area that could contain oil or gas, petroleum engineers begin their work, which includes determining the best location for drilling new wells, as well as the economic feasibility of developing them. They are also involved in operating oil and gas facilities, monitoring and forecasting reservoir performance, and utilizing enhanced oil recovery techniques that extend the life of wells. There are approximately 12,000 petroleum engineers employed in the United States.

History

Within a broad perspective, the history of petroleum engineering can be traced back hundreds of millions of years to when the remains of plants and animals blended with sand and mud and transformed into rock. It is from this ancient underground rock that petroleum is taken, for the organic matter of the plants and animals decomposed into oil during these millions of years and accumulated into pools deep underground.

In primitive times, people did not know how to drill for oil; instead, they collected the liquid substance after it had seeped to above-ground surfaces. Petroleum is known to have been used at that time for caulking ships and for concocting medicines.

Petroleum engineering as we know it today was not established until the mid-1800s, an incredibly long time after the fundamental ingredients of petroleum were deposited within the earth. In 1859, the American Edwin Drake was the first person to ever pump the so-called rock oil from under the ground, an endeavor that, before its success, was laughed at and considered impossible. Forward-thinking investors, however, had believed in the operation and thought that underground oil could be used as inexpensive fluid for lighting lamps and for lubricating machines (and therefore could make them rich). The drilling of the first well, in Titusville, Pennsylvania (1869), ushered in a new worldwide era: the oil age.

At the turn of the century, petroleum was being distilled into kerosene, lubricants, and wax. Gasoline was considered a useless by-product and was run off into rivers as waste. However, this changed with the invention of the internal combustion engine and the automobile. By 1915 there were more than half a million cars in the United States, virtually all of them powered by gasoline.

Edwin Drake's drilling operation struck oil 70 feet below the ground. Since that time, technological advances have been made, and the professional field of petroleum engineering has been established. Today's operations drill as far down as six miles. Because the United States began to rely so much on oil, the country contributed significantly to creating schools and educational programs in this engineering discipline. The world's first petroleum engineering curriculum was devised in the United States in 1914. Today there are 30 U.S. universities that offer petroleum engineering degrees.

The first schools were concerned mainly with developing effective methods of locating oil sites and with devising efficient machinery for drilling wells. Over the years, as sites have been depleted, engineers have been more concerned with formulating methods for extracting as much oil as possible from each well. Today's petroleum engineers focus on issues such as computerized drilling operations; however, because usually only about 40 to 60 percent of each site's oil is extracted, engineers must still deal with designing optimal conditions for maximum oil recovery.

The Job

Petroleum engineer is a rather generalized title that encompasses several specialties, each one playing an important role in ensuring the safe and productive recovery of oil and natural gas. In general, petroleum engineers are involved in the entire process of oil recovery, from preliminary steps, such as analyzing cost factors, to the last stages, such as monitoring the production rate and then repacking the well after it has been depleted.

Petroleum engineering is closely related to the separate engineering discipline of geoscience engineering. Before petroleum engineers can begin work on an oil reservoir, prospective sites must be sought by geological engineers, along with geologists and geophysicists. These scientists determine whether a site has potential oil. Petroleum engineers develop plans for drilling. Drilling is usually unsuccessful, with eight out of 10 test wells being "dusters" (dry wells) and only one of the remaining two test wells having enough oil to be commercially producible. When a significant amount of oil is discovered, engineers can begin their work of maximizing oil production at the site. The development company's engineering manager oversees the activities of the various petroleum engineering specialties, including reservoir engineers, drilling engineers, and production engineers.

Reservoir engineers use the data gathered by the previous geoscience studies and estimate the actual amount of oil that will be extracted from the reservoir. It is the reservoir engineers who determine whether the oil will be taken by primary methods (simply pumping the oil from the field) or by enhanced methods (using additional energy such as water pressure to force the oil up). The reservoir engineer is responsible for calculating the cost of the recovery process relative to the expected value of the oil produced, and simulates future performance using sophisticated computer models. Besides performing studies of existing company-owned oil fields, reservoir engineers also evaluate fields the company is thinking of buying.

Drilling engineers work with geologists and drilling contractors to design and supervise drilling operations. They are the engineers involved with the actual drilling of the well. They ask, What will be the best methods for penetrating the earth? It is the responsibility of these workers to supervise the building of the derrick (a platform, constructed over the well, that holds the hoisting devices), choose the equipment, and plan the drilling methods. Drilling engineers must have a thorough understanding of the geological sciences so that they can know, for instance, how much stress to place on the rock being drilled.

Production engineers determine the most efficient methods and equipment to optimize oil and gas production. For example, they establish the proper pumping unit configuration and perform tests to determine well fluid levels and pumping load. They plan field workovers and well stimulation techniques such as secondary and tertiary recovery (for example, injecting steam, water, or a special recovery fluid) to maximize field production.

Various research personnel are involved in this field; some are more specialized than others. They include the *research chief engineer,* who directs studies related to the design of new drilling and production methods, the *oil-well equipment research engineer,* who directs research to design improvements in oil-well machinery and devices, and the *oil-field equipment test engineer,* who conducts experiments to determine the effectiveness and safety of these improvements.

In addition to all of the above, sales personnel play an important part in the petroleum industry. *Oil-well equipment and services sales engineers* sell various types of equipment and devices used in all stages of oil recovery. They provide technical support and service to their clients, including oil companies and drilling contractors.

Requirements

High School

In high school, you can prepare for college engineering programs by taking courses in mathematics, physics, chemistry, geology, and computer science. Economics, history, and English are also highly recommended because these subjects will improve your communication and management skills. Mechanical drawing and foreign languages are also helpful.

Postsecondary Training

A bachelor's degree in engineering is the minimum requirement. In college, you can follow either a specific petroleum engineering curriculum or a program in a closely related field, such as geophysics or mining engineering. In the United States, there are 30 universities and colleges that offer programs that concentrate on petroleum engineering, many of which are located in California and Texas. The first two years toward the bachelor of science degree involve the study of many of the same subjects taken in high school, only at an advanced level, as well as basic engineering courses. In the junior and senior years, students take more specialized courses: geology, formation evaluation, properties of reservoir rocks and fluids, well drilling, properties of reservoir fluids, petroleum production, and reservoir analysis.

Because the technology changes so rapidly, many petroleum engineers continue their education to receive a master's degree and then a doctorate. Petroleum engineers who have earned advanced degrees command higher salaries and often are eligible for better advancement opportunities. Those who work in research and teaching positions are usually required to have these higher credentials.

Students considering an engineering career in the petroleum industry should be aware that the industry uses all kinds of engineers. People with chemical, electrical, geoscience, mechanical, environmental, and other engineering degrees are also employed in this field.

Certification or Licensing

Many jobs, including most public projects, require that the engineer be licensed as a professional engineer. To be licensed, candidates must have a degree from an engineering program accredited by the Accreditation Board for Engineering and Technology. Additional requirements for obtaining the P.E. license vary from state to state, but all applicants must take an exam and have several years of related experience on the job or in teaching.

Other Requirements

Students thinking about this career should enjoy science and math. You need to be a creative problem-solver who likes to come up with new ways to get things done and try them out. You need to be curious, wanting to know why and how things are done. You also need to be a logical thinker with a capacity for detail, and you must be a good communicator who can work well with others.

Exploring

One of the most satisfying ways to explore this occupation is to participate in Junior Engineering Technical Society (JETS) programs. JETS participants enter engineering design and problem-solving contests and learn team development skills, often with an engineering mentor. Science fairs and clubs also offer fun and challenging ways to learn about engineering.

Certain students are able to attend summer programs held at colleges and universities that focus on material not traditionally offered in high school. Usually these programs include recreational activities such as basketball, swimming, and track and field. For example, Worcester Polytechnic Institute offers the Frontiers program, a two-week residential session for high school seniors. The American Indian Science and Engineering Society also sponsors two- to six-week mathematics and science camps that are open to American Indian students and held at various college campuses.

Talking with someone who has worked as a petroleum engineer would also be a very helpful and inexpensive way of exploring this field. One good way to find an experienced person to talk to is through Internet sites that feature career areas to explore, industry message boards, and mailing lists.

You can also explore this career by touring oilfields or corporate sites (contact the public relations department of oil companies for more information), or you can try to land a temporary or summer job in the petroleum industry on a drilling and production crew. Trade journals, high school guidance counselors, the placement office at technical or community colleges, and the associations listed at the end of this article are other helpful resources that will help you learn more about the career of petroleum engineer.

Employers

Petroleum engineers are employed by major oil companies, as well as smaller oil companies. They work in oil exploration and production. Some petroleum engineers are employed by consulting companies and equipment suppliers. The federal government is also an employer of engineers. In the United States, oil or natural gas is produced in 33 states, with most sites located in Texas, Louisiana, Colorado, California, and Oklahoma, plus offshore regions. Many other engineers work in other oil-producing areas such as the Arctic Circle, China's Tarim Basin, and Saudi Arabia.

Starting Out

The most common and perhaps the most successful way to obtain a petroleum engineering job is to apply for positions through the student placement services department at the college you attend. Oil companies often have recruiters who seek potential graduates while they are in their last year of engineering school.

Applicants are also advised to simply check the job sections of major newspapers and apply directly to companies seeking employees. They should also keep informed of the general national employment outlook in this industry by reading trade and association journals, such as the Society of Petroleum Engineers' *Journal of Petroleum Technology*.

Engineering internships and co-op programs where students attend classes for a portion of the year and then work in an engineering-related job for the remainder of the year allow students to graduate with valuable work experience sought by employers. Many times these students are employed full-time after graduation at the place where they had their internship or co-op job.

As in most engineering professions, entry-level petroleum engineers first work under the supervision of experienced professionals for a number of years. New engineers usually are assigned to a field location where they learn different aspects of field petroleum engineering. Initial responsibilities may include well productivity, reservoir and enhanced recovery studies, production equipment and application design, efficiency analyses, and economic evaluations. Field assignments are followed by other opportunities in regional and headquarters offices.

Advancement

After several years working under professional supervision, engineers can begin to move up to higher levels. Workers often formulate a choice of direction during their first years on the job. In the operations division, petroleum engineers can work their way up from the field to district, division, and then operations manager. Some engineers work through various engineering positions from field engineer to staff, then division, and finally chief engineer on a project. Some engineers may advance into top executive management. In any position, however, continued enrollment in educational courses is usually required to keep abreast of technological progress and changes. After about four years of work experience, engineers usually apply for a P.E. license so they can be certified to work on a larger number of projects.

Others get their master's or doctoral degree so they can advance to more prestigious research engineering, university-level teaching, or consulting positions. Also, petroleum engineers may transfer to many other occupations, such as economics, environmental management, and groundwater hydrology. Finally, some entrepreneurial-minded workers become independent operators and owners of their own oil companies.

Earnings

Petroleum engineers with a bachelor's degree earned average starting salaries of $50,400 in 1999, according to the National Association of Colleges and Employers. A survey by the Society of Petroleum Engineers reports that its members earned an average salary of $93,013 in 2000. Petroleum engineers with a bachelor's degree earned an average salary of $90,858 in 2000, while those with a master's or doctorate earned $96,879. The survey also reports the following average salaries in 2000 for petroleum engineers by years of experience: 0 to 10 years, $66,254; 16 to 20 years, $95,130; and 26 or more years, $111,830.

Salary rates tend to reflect the economic health of the petroleum industry as a whole. When the price of oil is high, salaries can be expected to grow; low oil prices often result in stagnant wages.

Fringe benefits for petroleum engineers are good. Most employers provide health and accident insurance, sick pay, retirement plans, profit-sharing plans, and paid vacations. Education benefits are also competitive.

Work Environment

Petroleum engineers work all over the world: the high seas, remote jungles, vast deserts, plains, and mountain ranges. Petroleum engineers who are assigned to remote foreign locations may be separated from their families for long periods of time or be required to resettle their families when new job assignments arise. Those working overseas may live in company-supplied housing.

Some petroleum engineers, such as drilling engineers, work primarily out in the field at or near drilling sites in all kinds of weather and environments. The work can be dirty and dangerous. Responsibilities such as making reports, conducting studies of data, and analyzing costs are usually tended to in offices either away from the site or in temporary work trailers.

Other engineers work in offices in cities of varying sizes, with only occasional visits to an oil field. Research engineers work in laboratories much of the time, while those who work as professors spend most of their time on campuses. Workers involved in economics, management, consulting, and government service tend to spend their work time exclusively indoors.

Outlook

Employment for petroleum engineers is expected to decline through 2008. Despite this prediction, however, opportunities for petroleum engineers will exist because the number of degrees granted in petroleum engineering is low, leaving more job openings than there are qualified candidates. Additionally, employment opportunities may improve as a result of the Bush administration's plans to construct new gas refineries, pipelines, and transmission lines, as well as to drill in areas that were previously off-limits to such development.

The challenge for petroleum engineers in the past decade has been to develop technology that lets drilling and production be economically feasible even in the face of low oil prices. For example, engineers had to rethink how they worked in deep water. They used to believe deep wells would collapse if too much oil was pumped out at once. But the high costs of working in deep water plus low oil prices made low volumes uneconomical. So engineers learned how to boost oil flow by slowly upping the quantities wells pumped by improving valves, pipes, and other equipment used. Engineers have also cut the cost of deep-water oil and gas production in the Gulf of Mexico, predicted to be one of the most significant exploration hot spots in the world for the next decade, by placing wellheads on the ocean floor instead of on above-sea production platforms.

Cost-effective technology that permits new drilling and increases production will continue to be essential in the profitability of the oil industry. Therefore, petroleum engineers will continue to have a vital role to play, even in this age of streamlined operations and company restructurings.

For More Information

For information on careers in geology, contact:

American Association of Petroleum Geologists
PO Box 979
Tulsa, OK 74101-0979
Tel: 800-364-2274
Web: http://www.aapg.org

For information on summer programs, contact:

American Indian Science and Engineering Society
PO Box 9828
Albuquerque, NM 87119-9828
Tel: 505-765-1052
Web: http://www.aises.org/

For information about JETS programs and career brochures, contact:

Junior Engineering Technical Society (JETS)
1420 King Street, Suite 405
Alexandria, VA 22314
Tel: 703-548-5387
Email: jets@nae.edu
Web: http://www.jets.org

For a petroleum engineering career brochure, a list of petroleum engineering schools, and scholarship information, contact:

Society of Petroleum Engineers
PO Box 833836
Richardson, TX 75083-3836
Tel: 972-952-9393
Web: http://www.spe.org

For a Frontiers program brochure and application, contact:

Worcester Polytechnic Institute
100 Institute Road
Worcester, MA 01609-2280
Tel: 508-831-5000
Email: outreach@wpi.edu
Web: http://www.wpi.edu/Academics/Special/Outreach/Frontiers/

Petrologists

Overview

Geologists study the overall formation of the earth and its history, the movements of the earth's crust, and the mineral compositions and other natural resources. *Petrologists* focus specifically upon the analysis of the composition, structure, and history of rocks and rock formations. Petrologists are also interested in the formation of particular types of rocks that contain economically important materials such as gold, copper, and uranium. They also study the formation and composition of metals, precious stones, minerals, and meteorites, and they analyze a wide variety of substances, ranging from diamonds and gold to petroleum deposits that may be locked in rock formations beneath the earth's surface.

History

The field of petrology began to emerge in the early part of the 20th century as a subspecialty within geology. During this period, the mining of oil, coal, precious metals, uranium, and other substances increased rapidly. With the development of the gasoline engine in the mid-1950s, oil was the most significant raw material produced in the world, and the study of the earth's rock formations became invaluable to the mining of petroleum. In fact, the petroleum industry is the largest employer of petrologists; most are employed by one segment or another of the mining industry. Petrologists are also used in many other areas of mining and mineral extraction, and they are employed by numerous government agencies.

The Job

The major goal of petrology is to study the origin, composition, and history of rocks and rock formations. Because petrologists are intimately involved in the mining industry, they may work closely with the following types of scientists: geologists, who study the overall composition and structure of the earth as well as mineral deposits; *geophysicists,* who study the physical movements of the earth including seismic activity and physical properties of the earth and its atmosphere; *hydrologists,* who study the earth's waters and water systems; *mineralogists,* who examine and classify minerals and precious stones; and *paleontologists,* who study the fossilized remains of plants and animals found in geological formations.

Depending upon the type of work they do, petrologists may work frequently in teams with the many specialists previously mentioned. For example, in oil drilling they may work with geologists and geophysicists. The petrologist is responsible for analyzing rocks from bored samples beneath the earth's surface to determine the oil-bearing composition of rock samples as well as to determine whether certain rock formations are likely to have oil or natural gas content. In precious metal mining operations, petrologists may work closely with mineralogists. They may analyze core samples of mineral rock formations, called "mineral ore," while the mineralogists analyze in detail the specific mineral or minerals contained in such samples.

Because the surface of the earth is composed of thousands of layers of rock formations shaped over several billion years, the contents of these layers can be revealing, depending upon the rock and mineral composition of each respective layer. Each layer, or "stratum," of rock beneath the earth's surface tells a story of the earth's condition in the past and can reveal characteristics such as weather patterns, temperatures, the flow of water, the movement of glaciers, volcanic activity, and numerous other characteristics. These layers can also reveal the presence of minerals, mineral ores, and extractable fossil fuels such as petroleum and natural gas.

Petrologists spend time both in the field gathering samples and in the laboratory analyzing those samples. They use physical samples, photographs, maps, and diagrams to describe the characteristics of whatever formations they are analyzing. They use chemical compounds to break down rocks and rock materials to isolate certain elements. They use X rays, spectroscopic examination, electron microscopes, and other sophisticated means of testing and analyzing samples to isolate the specific components of various minerals and elements within the samples, in order to draw conclusions from their analysis.

Requirements

High School

If you are interested in petrology, you should focus your high school studies in the sciences and in mathematics. You will also want to take speech and English classes to hone your communication skills.

Postsecondary Training

Most professional positions in the field of petrology require a master's degree or a doctorate. Although individuals without these degrees can technically become petrologists, advances in the field and the profession's requirements will make it extremely difficult to enter the field without a graduate degree.

In college, you should concentrate your studies on the earth and physical sciences, geology, paleontology, mineralogy, and, of course, physics, chemistry, and mathematics. Because petrologists frequently analyze large volumes of data and write reports on such data, courses in computer science and English composition are advisable. Many students begin their careers in petrology by first majoring in geology or paleontology as an undergraduate and then, as graduate students, enter formal training in the field of petrology.

Certification or Licensing

Although no special certification exists for the field of petrology, several states require the registration of petrologists, and government petrologists may be required to take the civil service examination. The two major professional associations that provide information and continuing education to petrologists are the Geological Society of America and the American Association of Petroleum Geologists. The American Geological Institute publishes a directory that provides information concerning educational requirements for petrologists as well as schools offering formal training in this area.

Other Requirements

Requirements for this profession depend in large part upon the segment or subspecialty of the profession you choose. In some cases, petrologists work within a confined geographic area and spend most of their time in laboratories. In other instances, petrologists are called upon to travel throughout the United States and even overseas. Extensive travel is often required if you are working for a multinational oil company or other mining operation where you need to be available on short notice to analyze samples in various localities. Where important mining operations are undertaken, petrologists may be required to analyze rocks, ore, core samples, or other materials on short notice and under deadline pressure.

As with other scientific disciplines, teamwork is often an essential part of the job. Petrologists must be able to understand and relate to geologists, paleontologists, mineralogists, and other scientific experts; they must also be able to relate to and communicate their findings to supervisory personnel who may lack a strong technical background.

If you are considering petrology, you must be able to work well with others, as well as independently on various projects. You should also enjoy travel and the outdoors.

Exploring

If you are interested in pursuing this field, you may wish to meet and interview petrologists to find out more about the field. Petrologists may be found in universities and colleges that offer courses in geology and petrology, in certain government offices and field offices, and especially throughout the mining, oil, and natural gas industries.

Both geologists and petrologists require assistance in their work, and it is possible to obtain summer jobs and part-time employment in certain parts of the country where mining or oil exploration activities are taking place. For further information about the field of petrology and about various conferences in the geological professions, contact the American Geological Institute, the American Association of Petroleum Geologists, or the Geological Society of America.

Employers

Because much of the practice of petrology relates to the extraction of minerals, fossil fuels, metals, and natural resources, most petrologists work for petroleum and mining companies. Their work includes mining on the earth's surface, beneath the earth's surface, and under the ocean floor (in the case of offshore oil drilling, for example). Other petrologists work for federal, state, and local governments. In the federal branch, petrologists are often employed by the Environmental Protection Agency, the Department of Agriculture, the Department of Energy, the Department of Defense, the Department of Commerce, and the Department of the Interior. In fact, the largest government employer is the U.S. Geological Survey, a branch of the U.S. Department of the Interior. Other petrologists teach earth science classes in high schools, teach geology and petrology courses in colleges and universities, or work as consultants. In fact, the consulting industry is the most active employer and will probably remain so.

The field of petrology is open to a number of activities and subspecialties, and during their careers petrologists normally specialize in one area or another.

Starting Out

Both the federal government and state governments employ petrologists in various agencies. Thus, if you are undertaking graduate programs in petrology, you should contact both state civil service agencies in your respective state and the federal Office of Personnel Management (OPM). Federal agencies generally notify the OPM when they wish to fill vacancies in various positions and when new positions are created. The OPM has job information centers located in major cities throughout the United States. You can also obtain job information through the employment offices in your state's capital.

Although industrial firms do engage in campus recruiting, particularly for master's and doctoral level job applicants, less recruiting is occurring now than in the past. Thus, job seekers should not hesitate to contact oil exploration companies, mining companies, and other organizations directly. It is always a good idea to contact geologists and petrologists directly in various companies to learn about opportunities.

Part-time employment is available to geologists and petrologists in both private industry and various federal and state agencies. In some cases, agencies use volunteer students and scientists and pay only some expenses rather than a full salary. This arrangement may still be a good way to gain experience and to meet professionals in the field.

If you wish to teach petrology, you should consult college and university employment listings. For graduate students in the field, a limited number of part-time jobs as well as instructor-level jobs are available.

Note that junior high schools and high schools generally need more instructors in petrology than do colleges. This new reality reflects the fact that many high schools are beginning to offer a broader range of science courses. Individuals with a master's or doctoral degree are likely to be qualified to teach a variety of courses at the high school level, including earth science, physics, chemistry, mathematics, and biology.

Advancement

Because the level of competition in this field is keen and the oil industry is subject to fluctuation, those wishing to enter the petrology profession must think seriously about obtaining the highest level of education possible.

Advancement in the field generally involves spending a number of years as a staff scientist and then taking on supervisory and managerial responsibilities. The abilities to work on a team, to perform accurate and timely research, and to take charge of projects are all important for advancement in this field.

Because petrology, geology, and mineralogy are sciences that overlap, especially in industry, it is possible for petrologists to become mineralogists or geologists under the right circumstances. The fact that the three disciplines are intimately related can work to a person's advantage, particularly in changing economic times.

Earnings

Earnings for petrologists vary according to a person's educational attainment, experience, and ability. In 1999, according to a report by the National Association of Colleges and Employers, graduates holding a bachelor's degree in geology received salary offers averaging $34,900 a year. Those with a master's degree averaged $44,700. The U.S. Department of Labor reports that the median annual salary for geologists was $53,890 in 1998. The lowest paid 10 percent earned less than $30,950, while the highest paid 10 percent earned more than $101,390.

Petrologists employed by oil companies or consulting firms generally start at somewhat higher salaries than those who work for the government, but private industry favors those with master's or doctoral degrees.

Many petrologists are eligible to receive fringe benefits, such as life and health insurance, paid vacations, and pension plans.

Work Environment

Because the field of petrology involves a considerable amount of testing of rocks, ores, and other materials at mining sites and other types of geological sites, petrologists can expect to travel a considerable amount. In some cases, petrologists must travel back and forth from a field site to a laboratory several times while conducting a series of tests. If petrologists are working on exploratory investigations of a potential site for fuel, they may be at a remote location for weeks or months, until the data collected are sufficient to return to the laboratory. The conditions may be arduous, and leisure time may provide little to do on site.

The hours and working conditions of petrologists vary, but petrologists working in the field can generally expect long hours. Petrologists, geologists, and mineralogists frequently work in teams, and petrologists may work under the supervision of a head geologist, for example. In private industry, they also frequently work with mining engineers, mine supervisors, drilling supervisors, and others who are all part of a larger mining or drilling operation.

Outlook

The U.S. Department of Labor reports that employment opportunities for geologists, petrologists, and geophysicists will grow about as fast as the average for all occupations through 2008. A worldwide escalation in oil prices has spurred an increase in oil drilling and exploration. As a result, the number of new jobs in this field has increased, and the number of students who graduate with degrees in petrology or geology is on the rise. Additionally, environmental regulations will create a need for these scientists in environmental protection and reclamation work.

For More Information

For information on geology careers and job opportunities, contact the following organizations:

American Association of Petroleum Geologists
PO Box 979
Tulsa, OK 74101-0979
Tel: 800-364-2274
Web: http://www.aapg.org/indexaapg.html

American Geological Institute
4220 King Street
Alexandria, VA 22302-1502
Tel: 703-379-2480
Web: http://www.agiweb.org

Association of Engineering Geologists
Department of Geology & Geophysics
Texas A&M University, TAMU-3115
College Station, TX 77843-3115
Tel: 979-845-0142
Web: http://www.aegweb.org

Geological Society of America
PO Box 9140
3300 Penrose Place
Boulder, CO 80301-9140
Tel: 800-472-1988
Web: http://www.geosociety.org

Power Plant Workers

School Subjects

Mathematics
Technical/shop

Personal Skills

Mechanical/manipulative
Technical/scientific

Work Environment

Primarily indoors
Primarily one location

Minimum Education Level

High school diploma

Salary Range

$29,000 to $44,840 to $73,090+

Outlook

Little change or more slowly
than the average

Overview

Power plant workers include power plant operators, power distributors, and power dispatchers. In general, *power plant operators* control the machinery that generates electricity. *Power distributors* and *power dispatchers* oversee the flow of electricity through substations and a network of transmission and distribution lines to consumers. The generators in these power plants may produce electricity by converting energy from a nuclear reactor; burning oil, gas, or coal; or harnessing energy from falling water, the sun, or the wind. Approximately 45,000 power plant workers work in the United States.

History

The first permanent, commercial electric power-generating plant and distribution network was set up in New York City in 1882 under the supervision of the inventor Thomas Edison (1847-1931). Initially, the purpose of the network was to supply electricity to Manhattan buildings equipped with incandescent light bulbs, which had been developed just a few years earlier by Edison. Despite early problems in transmitting power over distance, the demand for electricity grew rapidly. Plant after plant was built to supply communities with electricity, and by 1900 incandescent lighting was a well-established part of urban life. Other uses of electric power were developed as well, and by about 1910 electric power became common in factories, public transportation systems, businesses, and homes.

Many early power plants generated electricity by harnessing water, or hydro, power. In hydroelectric plants, which are often located at dams on rivers, giant turbines are turned by falling water, and that energy is converted into electricity. Until the 1930s, hydroelectric plants supplied most electric power because hydro plants were less expensive to operate than plants that relied on thermal energy released by burning fuels such as coal. Afterwards, various technological advances made power generation in thermal plants more economical. Burning fossil fuels (coal, oil, or gas) creates heat, which is used to make steam to turn turbines and generate power. During the last several decades, many plants that use nuclear reactors as heat sources for making steam have been in operation.

Today, energy from all these sources—burning fossil fuels, nuclear reactors, and hydro power—is used to generate electricity. Large electric utility systems may generate power from different sources at multiple sites. While the essentials of generating, distributing, and utilizing electricity have been known for more than a century, the techniques and the equipment have changed. Over the years the equipment used in power generation and distribution has become much more sophisticated, efficient, and centralized, and the use of electric power exceeds the demand for workers.

The Job

Workers in power plants monitor and operate the machinery that generates electric power and sends power out to users in a network of distribution lines. Most employees work for electric utility companies or government agencies that produce power, but there are a small number who work for private companies that make electricity for their own use.

In general, power plant operators who work in plants fueled by coal, oil, or natural gas operate boilers, turbines, generators, and auxiliary equipment such as coal crushers. They also operate switches that control the amount of power created by the various generators and regulate the flow of power to outgoing transmission lines. They keep track of power demands on the system and respond to changes in demand by turning generators on and off and connecting and disconnecting circuits.

Operators must also watch meters and instruments and make frequent tests of the system to check power flow and voltage. They keep records of the load on the generators, power lines, and other equipment in the system, and they record switching operations and any problems or unusual situations that come up during their shifts.

In older plants, *auxiliary equipment operators* work throughout the plant monitoring specific kinds of equipment, such as pumps, fans, compressors, and condensers.

In newer plants, however, these workers have been mostly replaced by automated controls located in a central control room. *Central control room operators* and their assistants work in these nerve centers. Central control rooms are complex installations with many electronic instruments, meters, gauges, and switches that allow skilled operators to know exactly what is going on with the whole generating system and to quickly pinpoint any trouble that needs repairs or adjustments. In most cases, *control room mechanics* and *maintenance workers* are the ones who repair the equipment.

The electricity generated in power plants is sent through transmission lines to users at the direction of *load dispatchers*. Load dispatcher workrooms are command posts where the power generating and distributing activities are coordinated. Pilot boards in the workrooms are like automated maps that display what is going on throughout the entire distribution system. Dispatchers operate converters, transformers, and circuit breakers, based on readings given by monitoring equipment.

By studying factors, such as weather, that affect power use, dispatchers anticipate power needs and tell control room operators how much power will be needed to keep the power supply and demand in balance. If there is a failure in the distribution system, dispatchers redirect the power flow in transmission lines around the problem. They also operate equipment at substations, where the voltage of power in the system is adjusted.

Requirements

High School

Most employers prefer to hire high school graduates for positions in this occupational field, and often college-level training is desirable. If you are interested in this field, focus on obtaining a solid background in mathematics and science.

Postsecondary Training

Beginners in this field may start out as helpers or in laborer jobs, or they may begin training for duties in operations, maintenance, or other areas. Those who enter training for operator positions undergo extensive training by their employer, both on the job and in formal classroom settings. The training program is geared toward the particular plant in which they work and usually lasts several years. Even after they are fully qualified as operators or dispatchers, most employees will be required to take continuing education refresher courses.

Certification or Licensing

Power plants that generate electricity using nuclear reactors are regulated by the Nuclear Regulatory Commission (NRC). Operators in nuclear plants must be licensed by the NRC, as only licensed operators are authorized to control any equipment in the plant that affects the operation of the nuclear reactor. Nuclear reactor operators are also required to undertake regular drug testing.

Other Requirements

Although union membership is not necessarily a requirement for employment, many workers in power plants are members of either the International Brotherhood of Electrical Workers or the Utility Workers Union of America. Union members traditionally have been paid better than nonunion members.

Exploring

There is little opportunity for part-time or summer work experience in this field. However, many power plants (both nuclear and nonnuclear) have visitor centers where you can observe some of the power plant operations and learn about the various processes for converting energy into electricity. You might also locate information on this field at libraries, on the Internet, or by contacting the associations listed at the end of this article.

Employers

Employees in the power plant field work in several types of power-generating plants, including those that use natural gas, oil, coal, nuclear, hydro, solar, and wind energies. Because electric utility companies have dominated the energy field, most power plant workers work in electrical utilities. Government agencies that produce power are also employers, as are private companies that make electricity for their own use. Employment opportunities are available in any part of the country, as power plants are scattered nationwide.

Starting Out

People interested in working in electric power plants can contact local electric utility companies directly. Local offices of utility worker unions may also be sources of information about job opportunities. Leads for specific jobs may be found in newspaper classified ads and through the local offices of the state employment service. Graduates of technical training programs can often get help locating jobs from their schools' placement offices.

Advancement

After they have completed their training, power plant operators may move into supervisory positions, such as the position of a shift supervisor. Most opportunities for promotion are within the same plant or at other plants owned by the same utility company. With experience and appropriate training, nuclear power plant operators may advance to become senior reactor operators and shift supervisors.

Earnings

Salaries for workers in the utilities industry are relatively high but are based on skills and experience, geographical location, union status, and other factors. Operators in conventional (nonnuclear) power plants earned an average salary of $44,840 in 1998, according to the U.S. Department of Labor. The lowest paid 10 percent of workers earned less than $29,000, while the highest paid 10 percent earned more than $73,090 annually. Power distributors and dispatchers earned a median salary of $45,690 in 1998. Operators in nuclear power plants averaged $56,200 annually in 1998. In many cases, employee salaries are supplemented significantly by overtime pay. Overtime often becomes necessary during power outages and severe weather conditions.

Since power plants operate around the clock, employees work multiple shifts, which can last anywhere from four to 12 hours. In general, workers on night shifts are paid higher salaries than workers on day shifts. In addition to their regular earnings, most workers receive benefits, such as paid vacation days, paid sick leave, health insurance, and pension plans.

Work Environment

Most power plants are clean, well lighted, and ventilated. Some areas of the plant may be quite noisy. The work of power plant workers is not physically strenuous; workers usually sit or stand in one place as they perform their duties. Risk of falls, burns, and electric shock increases for those who work outside of the control room. Workers must follow strict safety regulations and sometimes wear protective clothing, such as hard hats and safety shoes, to ensure safety and avoid serious accidents.

Electricity is needed 24 hours a day, every day of the year, so power plants must be staffed at all times. Most workers will work some nights, weekends, and holidays, usually on a rotating basis, so that all employees share the stress and fatigue of working the more difficult shifts.

Outlook

Consumer demand for electric power is expected to increase in the next decade, but plants will install more automatic control systems and more efficient equipment, which should limit the growth of operating staffs. Employment opportunities may improve as a result of the Bush administration's plans to construct new electric and nuclear power generating plants.

Most job openings will develop when experienced workers retire or leave the field. Jobs in electric power plants are seldom affected by ups and downs in the economy, so employees in the field have rather stable jobs.

For More Information

For job listings and general information on the power industry, contact the following organizations:

American Public Power Association
2301 M Street, NW
Washington, DC 20037-1484
Tel: 202-467-2900
Web: http://www.appanet.org/

Edison Electric Institute
701 Pennsylvania Avenue, NW
Washington, DC 20004-2696
Tel: 202-508-5000
Web: http://www.eei.org

For information on union membership, contact the following organizations:

International Brotherhood of Electrical Workers
1125 15th Street, NW
Washington, DC 20005
Tel: 202-833-7000
Web: http://www.ibew.org

Utility Workers Union of America
815 16th Street, NW
Washington, DC 20006
Tel: 202-347-8105
Web: http://www.uwua.org/

Radiation Protection Technicians

	School Subjects
Mathematics Physics	
	Personal Skills
Mechanical/manipulative Technical/scientific	
	Work Environment
Indoors and outdoors Primarily one location	
	Minimum Education Level
Associate's degree	
	Salary Range
$25,000 to $34,372 to $42,000	
	Certification or Licensing
None available	
	Outlook
About as fast as the average	

Overview

Radiation protection technicians monitor radiation levels, protect workers, and decontaminate radioactive areas. They work under the supervision of nuclear scientists, engineers, or power plant managers and are trained in the applications of nuclear and radiation physics to detect, measure, and identify different kinds of nuclear radiation. They know federal regulations and permissible levels of radiation.

History

All forms of energy have the potential to endanger life and property if allowed to get out of control. This potential existed with the most primitive uses of fire, and it exists in the applications of nuclear power. Special care must be taken to prevent uncontrolled radiation in and around nuclear power plants. Skilled nuclear power plant technicians are among the workers who monitor and control radiation levels.

Around 1900, scientists discovered that certain elements give off invisible rays of energy. These elements are said to be radioactive, which means that they emit radiation. Antoine-Henri Becquerel (1852-1908), Marie Curie (1867-1934), and Pierre Curie (1859-1906) discovered and described chemical radiation before the turn of the century. In 1910, Marie Curie isolated pure radium, the most radioactive natural element, and in 1911 she was awarded the Nobel Prize for Chemistry for her work related to radiation.

Scientists eventually came to understand that radiation has existed in nature since the beginning of time, not only in specific elements on Earth, such as uranium, but also in the form of cosmic rays from outer space. All parts of the earth are constantly bombarded by a certain background level of radiation, which is considered normal or tolerable.

During the 20th century, research into the nature of radiation led to many controlled applications of radioactivity, ranging from X rays to nuclear weapons. One of the most significant of these applications, which has impacted our everyday life, is the use of nuclear fuel to produce energy. Nuclear power reactors produce heat that is used to generate electricity.

The biological effects of radiation exposure continue to be studied, but we know that short-term effects include nausea, hemorrhaging, and fatigue; long-range and more dangerous effects include cancer, lowered fertility, and possible birth defects. These factors have made it absolutely clear that if radiation energy is to be used for any purpose, the entire process must be controlled. Thus, appropriate methods of radiation protection and monitoring have been developed; it is the radiation protection technician's job to insure that these methods are accurately and consistently employed.

The Job

Radiation protection technicians protect workers, the general public, and the environment from overexposure to radiation. Many of their activities are highly technical in nature: they measure radiation and radioactivity levels in work areas and in the environment by collecting samples of air, water, soil, plants, and other materials; record test results and inform the appropriate personnel when tests reveal deviations from acceptable levels; help power plant workers set up equipment that automatically monitors processes within the plant and records deviations from established radiation limits; and calibrate and maintain such equipment using hand tools.

Radiation protection technicians work efficiently with people of different technical backgrounds. They instruct operations personnel in making the necessary adjustments to correct problems such as excessive radiation levels, discharges of radionuclide materials above acceptable levels, or improper chemical levels. They also prepare reports for supervisory and regulatory agencies.

Radiation protection technicians are concerned with ionizing radiation, particularly three types known by the Greek words: *alpha, beta,* and *gamma.* Ionization occurs when atoms split and produce charged particles. If these particles strike the cells in the body, they cause damage by upsetting well-ordered chemical processes.

In addition to understanding the nature and effects of radiation, technicians working in nuclear power plants understand the principles of nuclear power plant systems. They have a thorough knowledge of the instrumentation used to monitor radiation in every part of the plant and its immediate surroundings. They also play an important role in educating other workers about radiation monitoring and control.

Radiation protection technicians deal with three basic radiation concepts: time, distance from the radiation source, and shielding. When considering time, technicians know that certain radioactive materials break down into stable elements in a matter of days or even minutes. Other materials, however, continue to emit radioactive particles for thousands of years. Radiation becomes less intense in proportion to its distance from the source, so distance is an important concept in controlling radiation exposure. Shielding is used to protect people from radiation exposure. Appropriate materials with a specific thickness must be used to block emission of radioactive particles.

Because radiation generally cannot be seen, heard, or felt, radiation protection technicians use special instruments to detect and measure it and to determine the extent of radiation exposure. Technicians use devices that measure the ionizing effect of radiation on matter to determine the presence of radiation and, depending on the instrument used, the degree of radiation danger in a given situation.

Two such devices are Geiger counters and dosimeters, which measure received radiation doses. Dosimeters are often in the form of photographic badges worn by personnel and visitors. These badges are able to detect radioactivity because it shows up on photographic film. Radiation protection technicians calculate the amount of time that personnel may safely work in contaminated areas, considering maximum radiation exposure limits and the radiation level in the particular area. They also use specialized equipment to detect and analyze radiation levels and chemical imbalances.

Finally, although the radiation that is released into the environment surrounding a nuclear facility is generally far less than that released through background radiation sources, radiation protection technicians must be prepared to monitor people and environments during abnormal situations and emergencies.

Under normal working conditions, technicians monitor the workforce, the plant, and the nearby environment for radioactive contamination; test plant workers for radiation exposure, both internally and externally; train personnel in the proper use of monitoring and safety equipment; help *nuclear materials handling technicians* prepare and monitor radioactive waste shipments; perform basic radiation orientation training; take radiation contamination and control surveys, air sample surveys, and radiation level surveys; maintain and calibrate radiation detection instruments using standard samples to determine accuracy; ensure that radiation protection regulations, standards, and procedures are followed and records kept of all regular measurements and radioactivity tests; and carry out decontamination procedures that ensure the safety of plant workers and the continued operation of the plant.

Requirements

High School

You should have a solid background in basic high school mathematics and science. Take four years of English, at least two years of mathematics including algebra, and at least one year of physical science, preferably physics with laboratory instruction. Computer programming and applications, vocational machine shop operations, and blueprint reading will also provide you with a good foundation for further studies.

Postsecondary Training

After high school, you will need to study at a two-year technical school or community college. Several public or private technical colleges offer programs designed to prepare nuclear power plant radiation protection technicians. Other programs, called nuclear technology or nuclear materials handling technology, also provide a good foundation. You should be prepared to spend from one to two years in postsecondary technical training taking courses in chemistry, physics, laboratory procedures, and technical writing. Because the job entails accurately recording important data and writing clear, concise technical reports, technicians need excellent writing skills.

A typical first year of study for radiation protection technicians includes introduction to nuclear technology, radiation physics, mathematics, electricity and electronics, technical communications, radiation detection and measurement, inorganic chemistry, radiation protection, blueprint reading, quality assurance/quality control, nuclear systems, computer applications, and radiation biology.

Course work in the second year includes technical writing, advanced radiation protection, applied nuclear chemistry, radiological emergencies, advanced chemistry, radiation shielding, radiation monitoring techniques, advanced radionuclide analysis, occupational safety and health, nuclear systems and safety, radioactive materials disposal and management, and industrial economics.

Students who graduate from nuclear technician programs are usually hired by nuclear power plants and other companies and institutions involved in nuclear-related activities. These employers provide a general orientation to their operations and further training specific to their procedures.

Certification or Licensing

At present, there are no special requirements for licensing or certification of nuclear power plant radiation protection technicians. Some graduates of radiation control technology programs, however, may want to become nuclear materials handling technicians. For this job, licensing may be required, but the employer usually will arrange for the special study needed to pass the licensing test.

Other Requirements

Federal security clearances are required for workers in jobs that involve national security. Nuclear Regulatory Commission (NRC) clearance is required for both government and private industry employees in securing related positions. Certain projects may necessitate military clearance with or without NRC clearance. Employers usually help arrange such clearances.

Exploring

Your school's vocational guidance counselor can help you learn more about this occupation. You also can obtain information from the occupational information centers at community and technical colleges.

Your science teacher may be able to arrange field trips and invite speakers to describe various careers. Nuclear reactor facilities are unlikely to provide tours, but they may be able to furnish literature on radiation physics and radiation control. Radiation protection technicians employed at nuclear-related facilities may be invited to speak about their chosen field.

Radiation is used for medical diagnosis and treatment in hospitals all over the country. Radiology departments of local hospitals often provide speakers for science or career classes.

In addition, a utilities company with a nuclear-fired plant may be able to offer you a tour of the visitor's center at the plant, where much interesting and valuable information about nuclear power plant operation is available. Small reactors used for experiments, usually affiliated with universities and research centers, also may give tours.

Employers

Radiation protection technicians are employed by government agencies, such as the Department of Energy and the Department of Defense, as well as electric power utilities that operate nuclear plants. Other than utilities, technicians are employed by nuclear materials handling and processing facilities, regulatory agencies, nondestructive testing firms, radiopharmaceutical industries, nuclear waste handling facilities, nuclear service firms, and national research laboratories.

Starting Out

The best way to enter this career is to graduate from a radiation control technology program and make use of the school's placement office to find that first job. Another excellent way to enter the career is to join the U.S. Navy and enter its technical training program for various nuclear specialties.

Graduates of radiation control technology programs are usually interviewed and recruited while in school by representatives of companies with nuclear facilities. At that time, they may be hired with arrangements made to begin work soon after graduation. Graduates from strong programs may receive several attractive job offers.

Entry-level jobs for graduate radiation protection technicians are varied and numerous. *Radiation monitors* are involved in personnel monitoring, decontaminating, and area monitoring and reporting. Another entry-level job is *instrument calibration technician.* These technicians test instrument reliability, maintain standard sources, and adjust and calibrate instruments. *Accelerator safety technicians* evaluate nuclear accelerator operating procedures and shielding to ensure personnel safety. *Radiobiology technicians* test the external and internal effects of radiation in plants and animals, collect data on facilities where potential human exposure to radiation exists, and recommend improvements in techniques or facilities.

Hot-cell operators conduct experimental design and performance tests involving materials of very high radioactivity. *Environmental survey technicians* gather and prepare radioactive samples from air, water, and food specimens. They may handle nonradioactive test specimens for test comparisons with National Environmental Policy Act standards. *Reactor safety technicians* study personnel safety through the analysis of reactor procedures and shielding and through analysis of radioactivity tests.

Advancement

A variety of positions are available for experienced and well-trained radiation protection technicians. *Research technicians* develop new ideas and techniques in the radiation and nuclear field. *Instrument design technicians* design and prepare specifications and tests for use in advanced radiation instrumentation. *Customer service specialists* work in sales, installation, modification, and maintenance of customers' radiation control equipment. *Radiochemistry technicians* prepare and analyze new and old compounds, utilizing the latest equipment and techniques. *Health physics technicians* train new radiation monitors, analyze existing procedures, and conduct tests of experimental design and radiation safety. *Soils evaluation technicians* assess soil density, radioactivity, and moisture content to determine sources of unusually high levels of radioactivity. *Radioactive waste analysts* develop waste disposal techniques, inventory stored waste, and prepare waste for disposal.

Some of the most attractive opportunities for experienced radiation protection technicians include working as radiation experts or consultants for a company or laboratory. Consultants may work for nuclear engineering or nuclear industry consulting firms or manage their own consulting businesses.

Earnings

The earnings of radiation protection technicians who are beginning their careers depend on what radiation safety program they work in (nuclear power, federal or state agencies, research laboratories, medical facilities, etc.). They may begin as salaried staff or be paid hourly wages. Technicians who receive hourly wages usually work in shifts and receive premium pay for overtime.

Trained technicians earn annual starting salaries of up to $25,000 a year. After three to five years of experience, they can expect to earn as much as $33,000 a year. Consultants may earn as much as $42,000 a year. Average annual earnings for radiation protection technicians were $34,372 in 1998, according to the *O*NET Dictionary of Occupational Titles.* Earnings are also affected by whether technicians remain in their entry-level jobs or become supervisors and whether they are able to pass a national competency test that makes them a Nationally Registered Radiation Protection Technologist.

Technicians usually receive benefits, such as paid holidays and vacations, insurance plans, and retirement plans. Because of the rapid changes that occur in the radiation safety industry, many employers pay for job-related study and participation in workshops, seminars, and conferences.

Work Environment

Depending on the employer, work environments vary from offices and control rooms to relatively cramped and cold areas of power plants.

Of all power plant employees, radiation protection technicians are perhaps best able to evaluate and protect against the radiation hazards that are an occupational risk of this field. The safety of all plant workers depends on the quality and accuracy of their work.

Radiation protection technicians wear film badges or carry pocket monitors to measure their exposure to radiation. Like all other nuclear power plant employees, technicians wear safety clothing, and radiation-resistant clothing may be required in some areas. This type of clothing contains materials that reduce the level of radiation before it reaches the human body.

In some of the work done by radiation protection technicians, radiation shielding materials, such as lead and concrete, are used to enclose radioactive materials while the technician manipulates these materials from outside the contaminated area. These procedures are called hot-cell operations. In some areas, automatic alarm systems are used to warn of radiation hazards so that proper protection can be maintained.

The career of a radiation protection technician is very demanding. Technicians must have confidence in their ability to measure and manage potentially dangerous radioactivity on a daily basis. Radiation protection technicians play an important teaching role in the nuclear energy-fueled power plant. They must know the control measures required for every employee and be capable of explaining the reasons for such measures. Because abnormal conditions sometimes develop in the nuclear power industry, technicians must be able to withstand the stress, work long hours without making mistakes, and participate as a cooperating member of a team of experts.

Successful technicians are usually individuals who are able to confidently accept responsibility, communicate effectively in person and on paper, and enjoy doing precise work. Their participation is vital to the successful application of nuclear technology.

Outlook

As of 2001, there were 103 nuclear power plants licensed to operate in 32 states of the United States. In an effort to offset the effects of rising costs to the public for energy obtained from traditional resources, some government officials are calling for the construction of new nuclear power plants and the relicensing of existing ones. If these plants are constructed and existing plants are relicensed, radiation protection engineers will enjoy increased employment opportunities.

However, even if the nuclear power industry experiences a decline, the employment outlook for radiation protection technicians should remain strong. Technicians are needed to support radiation safety programs in Department of Energy facilities, Department of Defense facilities, hospitals, universities, state regulatory programs, federal regulatory agencies, and many industrial activities. New technicians will be needed to replace retiring technicians or technicians who leave the field for other reasons. Increased efforts to enforce and improve safety standards may also result in new jobs for technicians. Because radiation programs have been in development for half a century, most of the radiation safety programs are well-established and rely primarily on technicians to keep them running.

For More Information

For information on careers, publications, scholarships, and seminars, contact:

American Nuclear Society
555 North Kensington Avenue
LaGrange Park, IL 60526
Tel: 708-352-6611
Web: http://www.ans.org

This professional organization of more than 6,000 members promotes the practice of radiation safety. For information on the latest issues, radiation facts, and membership, contact:

Health Physics Society
1313 Dolley Madison Boulevard, Suite 402
McLean, VA 22101
Tel: 703-790-1745
Web: http://www.hps.org

This organization is dedicated to the peaceful use of nuclear technologies. To read Careers and Education: Your Bright Future in Nuclear Energy and Technology, *check out the Web site or contact:*

Nuclear Energy Institute
1776 I Street, NW, Suite 400
Washington, DC 20006-3708
Tel: 202-739-8000
Web: http://www.nei.org/

Surveyors

Geography Mathematics	School Subjects
Communication/ideas Technical/scientific	Personal Skills
Primarily outdoors Primarily multiple locations	Work Environment
Some postsecondary training	Minimum Education Level
$21,510 to $37,640 to $76,880+	Salary Range
Required by all states	Certification or Licensing
About as fast as the average	Outlook

Overview

Surveyors mark exact measurements and locations of elevations, points, lines, and contours on or near Earth's surface. They measure distances between points to determine property boundaries and to provide data for mapmaking, construction projects, and other engineering purposes. There are approximately 110,000 surveying workers employed in the United States.

History

As the United States expanded from the Atlantic to the Pacific, people moved over the mountains and plains into the uncharted regions of the West. They found it necessary to chart their routes and to mark property lines and borderlines by surveying and filing claims.

The need for accurate geographical measurements and precise records of those measurements has increased over the years: for the location of a trail, highway, or road; the site of a log cabin, frame house, or skyscraper; the right-of-way for water pipes, drainage ditches, and telephone lines; and for the charting of unexplored regions, bodies of water, land, and underground mines.

As a result, the demand for professional surveyors has grown and become more complex. New computerized systems are now used to more accurately and efficiently map, store, and retrieve locational data. This new technology has not only improved the process of surveying but extended its reach as well. Surveyors can now make detailed maps of ocean floors and the moon's surface.

The Job

On proposed construction projects, such as highways, airstrips, and housing developments, it is the surveyor's responsibility to make necessary measurements through an accurate and detailed survey of the area. The surveyor usually works with a field party consisting of several people. *Instrument assistants,* also called *surveying and mapping technicians,* handle a variety of surveying instruments including the theodolite, transit, level, surveyor's chain, rod, and other electronic equipment. In the course of the survey, it is important that all readings be accurately recorded and field notes maintained so that the survey can be checked for accuracy.

Surveyors may specialize in one or more particular types of surveying:

Land surveyors establish township, property, and other tract-of-land boundary lines. Using maps, notes, or actual land title deeds, they survey the land, checking for the accuracy of existing records. This information is used to prepare legal documents such as deeds and leases. *Land surveying managers* coordinate the work of surveyors, their parties, and legal, engineering, architectural, and other staff involved in a project. In addition, these managers develop policy, prepare budgets, certify work upon completion, and handle numerous other administrative duties.

Highway surveyors establish grades, lines, and other points of reference for highway construction projects. This survey information is essential to the work of the numerous engineers and the construction crews who build the new highway.

Geodetic surveyors measure large masses of land, sea, and space that must take into account the curvature of Earth and its geophysical characteristics. Their work is helpful in establishing points of reference for smaller land surveys, determining national boundaries, and preparing maps. *Geodetic computers* calculate latitude, longitude, angles, areas, and other information needed for mapmaking. They work from field notes made by an engineering survey party and also use reference tables and a calculating machine or computer.

Marine surveyors measure harbors, rivers, and other bodies of water. They determine the depth of the water through measuring sound waves in relation to nearby land masses. Their work is essential for planning and constructing navigation projects, such as breakwaters, dams, piers, marinas, and bridges, and preparing nautical charts and maps.

Mine surveyors make surface and underground surveys, preparing maps of mines and mining operations. Such maps are helpful in examining underground passages within the levels of a mine and assessing the volume and location of raw material available.

Geophysical prospecting surveyors locate and mark sites considered likely to contain petroleum deposits. *Oil-well directional surveyors* use sonic, electronic, and nuclear measuring instruments to gauge the presence and amount of oil- and gas-bearing reservoirs. *Pipeline surveyors* determine rights-of-way for oil construction projects, providing information essential to the preparation for and laying of the lines.

Photogrammetric engineers determine the contour of an area to show elevations and depressions and indicate such features as mountains, lakes, rivers, forests, roads, farms, buildings, and other landmarks. Aerial, land, and water photographs are taken with special equipment able to capture images of very large areas. From these pictures, accurate measurements of the terrain and surface features can be made. These surveys are helpful in construction projects and the preparation of topographical maps. Photogrammetry is particularly helpful in charting areas that are inaccessible or difficult to travel.

Requirements

High School

If you are interested in a career as a surveyor, you should take algebra, geometry, trigonometry, physics, mechanical drawing, and other related science or drafting courses in high school. If available, take computer science classes to prepare yourself for working with technical surveying equipment.

Postsecondary Training

Depending on state requirements, you will need some amount of postsecondary education. The quickest route is by earning a bachelor's degree in surveying or engineering combined with on-the-job training. Other entry options include obtaining more job experience combined with a one- to three-year program in surveying and surveying technology offered by community colleges, technical institutes, and vocational schools.

Certification or Licensing

All 50 states require that surveyors making property and boundary surveys be licensed or registered. The requirements for licensure vary, but most require a degree in surveying or a related field, a certain number of years of experience, and examinations in land surveying. Generally, the higher the degree obtained, the less experience required. Those with bachelor's degrees may only need two to four years of on-the-job experience, while those with a lesser degree may need up to 12 years of prior experience to obtain a license. Information on specific requirements can be obtained by contacting the licensure department of the state in which you plan to work. If you are seeking employment in the federal government, you must take a civil service examination and meet the educational, experience, and other specified requirements for the position.

Other Requirements

The ability to work with numbers and perform mathematical computations accurately and quickly is very important. Other helpful qualities are the ability to visualize and understand objects in two and three dimensions (spatial relationships) and to discriminate between and compare shapes, sizes, lines, shadings, and other forms (form perception).

Surveyors walk a great deal and carry equipment over all types of terrain so endurance and coordination are important physical assets. In addition, surveyors direct and supervise the work of their team so you should be good at working with other people and demonstrate leadership abilities.

Exploring

One of the best opportunities for experience is a summer job with a construction outfit or company that requires survey work. Even if the job does not involve direct contact with survey crews, it will offer an opportunity to observe surveyors and talk with them about their work. Some colleges have work-study programs that offer on-the-job experience. These opportunities, like summer or part-time jobs, provide helpful contacts in the field that may lead to future full-time employment.

Employers

According to 1998 data from the U.S. Department of Labor, 64 percent of the estimated 110,000 surveying workers in the United States are employed in engineering, architectural, and surveying firms. Federal, state, and local government agencies employ 17 percent, and the majority of the remaining surveyors work for construction firms, oil and gas extraction companies, and public utilities. Approximately 6,800 surveyors are self-employed.

Starting Out

Apprentices with a high school education can enter the field as equipment operators or surveying assistants. Those who have postsecondary education can enter the field more easily, beginning as surveying and mapping technicians.

College graduates can learn about job openings through their schools' placement services or through potential employers that may visit their campus. Many cities have employment agencies specializing in seeking out workers for positions in surveying and related fields. Check your local newspaper or telephone book to see if such recruiting firms exist in your area.

Advancement

With experience, workers advance through the leadership ranks within a surveying team. Workers begin as assistants, then can move into positions such as senior technician, party chief, and, finally, licensed surveyor. Because surveying work is closely related to other fields, surveyors can move into electrical, mechanical, or chemical engineering or specialize in drafting.

Earnings

In 1998, surveyors earned a median annual salary of $37,640. According to the *Occupational Outlook Handbook,* the middle 50 percent earned between $27,580 and $50,380 a year. The lowest paid 10 percent were paid less than $21,510, and the highest paid 10 percent earned over $76,880 a year. In general, the federal government paid the highest wages to its surveyors, $52,400 a year.

Most positions with the federal, state, and local governments and with private firms provide life and medical insurance, pension, vacation, and holiday benefits.

Work Environment

Surveyors work 40-hour weeks except when overtime is necessary to meet a project deadline. The peak work period is during the summer months when weather conditions are most favorable. However, it is not uncommon for the surveyor to be exposed to adverse weather conditions.

Some survey projects involve a certain amount of hazardous conditions, depending upon the region and climate as well as the plant and animal life. Survey crews may encounter snakes, poison ivy, and other plant and animal life and may suffer heat exhaustion, sunburn, and frostbite while on the field. Survey projects, particularly those near construction projects or busy highways, may impose dangers of injury from heavy traffic, flying objects, and other accidental hazards. Unless the surveyor is employed only for office assignments, the work location most likely will change from survey to survey. Some assignments may necessitate being away from home for periods of time.

Outlook

The U.S. Department of Labor predicts the employment of surveyors to grow about as fast as the average for all occupations through 2008. The constant need to replace workers who leave the workforce to retire or switch occupations will continue to provide employment opportunities. The outlook is best for surveyors who have college degrees and advanced field experience. In addition, the widespread use of advanced technology, such as the Global Positioning System and Geographic Information System, will provide jobs to surveyors with strong technical knowledge and computer skills.

Growth in urban and suburban areas—with the need for new streets, homes, shopping centers, schools, and gas and water lines—will provide many employment opportunities. State and federal highway improvement programs and local urban redevelopment programs also will provide jobs for surveyors. The expansion of industrial and business firms and the relocation of some firms to large undeveloped tracts will also create job openings. However, construction projects are closely tied to the state of the economy, so employment may fluctuate from year to year.

For More Information

For information on careers, continuing education, and scholarship opportunities, contact the following organizations:

American Congress on Surveying and Mapping
6 Montgomery Village Avenue, Suite #403
Gaithersburg, MD 20879
Tel: 240-632-9716
Web: http://www.acsm.net

American Society for Photogrammetry and Remote Sensing
5410 Grosvenor Lane, Suite 210
Bethesda, MD 20814-2160
Tel: 301-493-0290
Email: asprs@asprs.org
Web: http://www.asprs.org

Additional Careers

The following careers represent other opportunities in the energy industry:

Geological technicians. Geological technicians assist geologists in their studies of the earth's physical makeup and history. This includes the exploration of a wide variety of phenomena, such as mountain uplifting, rock formations, mineral deposition, earthquakes, and volcanic eruptions. Modern geology is particularly concerned with the exploration for mineral and petroleum deposits in the earth and with minimizing the effects of manmade structures on the environment.

Metallurgical technicians. Metallurgy involves processing and converting metals into usable forms. Metallurgical technicians work in support of metallurgical engineers, metallurgists, and materials scientists. These jobs involve the production, quality control, and experimental study of metals. Metallurgical technicians may conduct tests on the properties of metals, develop and modify test procedures and equipment, analyze data, and prepare reports. During recent years, metallurgists have extended their research to include nonmetallic materials such as ceramics, glass, plastics, and semiconductors. The field of study has grown so broad that it is sometimes referred to as materials science, and technicians are called *materials science technicians*.

Meter readers, utilities. Meter readers check the level of gas, water, steam, and electricity consumption in homes and businesses by going from building to building and reading meters that measure how much energy has been used. They then record this amount in a route book or with an electronic, hand-held device. Meter readers are also responsible for checking the meters and connection lines for damage or signs of tampering and for turning on and shutting off utility service.

Mining engineers. Mining engineers deal with the exploration, location, and planning for removal of minerals and mineral deposits from the earth. These include metals (iron, copper), nonmetallic minerals (limestone, gypsum), and coal. Mining engineers conduct preliminary surveys of mineral deposits and examine them to ascertain whether they can be extracted efficiently and economically, using either underground or surface mining methods. They plan and design the development of mine shafts and tunnels, devise means of extracting minerals, and select the methods to be used in transporting the minerals to the surface. They supervise all mining operations and are responsible for mine safety. Mining engineers normally specialize in design, research and development, or production.

Petroleum technicians. Petroleum technicians work in a wide variety of specialties. Many kinds of drilling technicians drill for petroleum from the earth and beneath the ocean. *Loggers* analyze rock cuttings from drilling and measure characteristics of rock layers. Various types of *production technicians* "complete" wells (prepare wells for production), collect petroleum from producing wells, and control production. *Engineering technicians* help improve drilling technology, maximize field production, and provide technical assistance. *Maintenance technicians* keep machinery and equipment running smoothly.

Renewable energy careers. Renewable energy resources include wind and solar power, hydropower, bioenergy, and geothermal energy. **Wind energy** is harvested using a wind turbine. The wind industry is growing at a rate of 25 percent per year, according to the National Renewable Energy Laboratory (NREL). Numerous technologies are available to harness the energy of the sun, known as **solar power.** The most common of these technologies used in the United States include solar thermal electric systems, solar hot water systems, photovoltaics, and passive solar building design. Solar power, while not used as frequently in the United States as in the rest of the world, is growing in popularity. Solar hot water systems are used in schools, hospitals, prisons, and residential swimming pools. **Hydropower** uses the energy of flowing water to create electricity. It is the largest and least expensive type of renewable energy produced in the United States, according to the NREL. **Bioenergy** is energy that is stored in organic matter, or biomass. Biomass fuels are used to heat buildings (using wood or straw), produce electricity (using wood waste), and develop transportation fuels (using corn-based ethanol). According to the NREL, biomass is the second largest source of renewable energy in the world. **Geothermal energy** is heat from the earth that warms water in underground reservoirs. This water, depending on its temperature, can be used to grow crops, heat and cool buildings, and melt snow on sidewalks. Workers from disciplines as varied as architecture, sales, earth science, design, marketing, biology, engineering, and construction are employed by these industries.

Roustabouts. Roustabouts do the routine physical labor and maintenance around oil wells, pipelines, and natural gas facilities. Sample tasks include clearing trees and brush, mixing concrete, manually loading and unloading pipe and other materials onto or from trucks or boats, and assembling pumps, boilers, valves, and steam engines and performing minor repairs on such equipment.

Surveying and mapping technicians. Surveying and mapping technicians help determine, describe, and record geographic areas or features. They are usually the leading assistant to the professional surveyor, civil engineer, or mapmaker. They operate modern surveying and mapping instruments and may participate in other operations. Technicians must have a basic knowledge of the current practices and legal implications of surveys to establish and record property size, shape, topography, and boundaries.

Index